The Taming of
GOVERNMENT

The Taming of GOVERNMENT

Micro/macro disciplines on Whitehall and Town Hall

Government the culprit

Bureaucracy • Budgeting
Disarming the Treasury • Constitutional reform
Do-it-yourself 'cutting' by pricing

STEPHEN C. LITTLECHILD   GORDON TULLOCK

A. P. L. MINFORD   ARTHUR SELDON   ALAN BUDD

CHARLES K. ROWLEY

With an Introduction by
LORD ROBBINS

First published by
THE INSTITUTE OF ECONOMIC AFFAIRS
1979

C 49574

First published in September 1979 by
THE INSTITUTE OF ECONOMIC AFFAIRS
© The Institute of Economic Affairs 1979

Printed in England by
Goron Pro-Print Co. Ltd., Lancing, Sussex
Set in Monotype Times Roman 11 on 12 point

Contents

Contents

Preface

The *IEA Readings* have been devised to refine the market in economic thinking by presenting differing aspects of a single theme in one volume. They are intended primarily for teachers and students of economics but are edited for non-economists in industry and government who want to know how economics can explain their activities.

Readings 21 is the latest in a series of IEA studies that have examined the economics of government. This study concentrates on the tendency of government to become too big and its causes, consequences and cures. It is based on a Seminar held in London on 6 April 1979, which brought together economists of varying approaches to the subject, ranging from what might be regarded as the conventional study of the financial/fiscal powers of government over the economy to the latest development of the economics of bureaucracy, and including micro- as well as macro-economic controls on government.

Disciplining government

The Seminar was opened by Professor Lord Robbins, who has chaired several notable IEA Seminars. As a student of the history of economic thought on the functions of government, his introductory remarks were especially authoritative. He emphasised that by 'taming' government he understood disciplining rather than destroying it—making it useful rather than harmful. The classical economists had earnestly discussed the necessary functions of government, and an early formulation of Adam Smith in 1776 had been re-stated in uncannily similar language by J. M. Keynes in 1932. The task was to decide which functions had to be performed by government and which could be better left to individuals or private organisations engaging in voluntary exchange in the market. But Lord Robbins emphasised that over the last century or more government has expanded far beyond what Adam Smith or Keynes had contemplated. It had created monopolies and privileges, imposed dis-incentives and disruptions. It had created a shortage of housing and kept alive industry that was devouring resources that could be used better

ix

elsewhere. It had debauched the value of money. In all, government had intruded into functions where it was not only inferior to decentralised private activities but had moreover discouraged or inhibited them. The aim was to ensure that government restricted itself to promoting rather than usurping the creative activities of private citizens. We had proceeded dangerously far in these directions, and their reversal would require persuasive ingenuity and time based on the right ideas on the functions of government.

Government—cure or cause of *malaise*?

The opening paper was an incisive review by Professor Stephen Littlechild of the three broad phases in the approach of economists to the functions and powers of government. The first phase, that of the classical economists in the early 19th century, showed scepticism of the power of government and arrived at proposals for policy that reflected this attitude.

The second phase, which began in the second half of the 19th century and has extended to recent times, took a much more charitable and romantic view of the capabilities and intentions of men in government. In language familiar to economists, it made some very heroic assumptions about human nature, about the working of political institutions, and about the intention and capacity of politicians to serve 'the public interest', and the sea-green incorruptibility of public officials. Hence the stream of apparently divergent but basically common doctrines on the functions of government—from the Fabians in the 1880s, through the municipal Conservatives of the early 19th century, to Keynes in the 1930s, and Beveridge, Butler and Bevan in the war and post-war years. Whatever their differences in the departments of public policy, they all ended with proposals for the enlargement of the functions and power of government based on the implicit but unquestioned assumption that government could do good, and would repair the errors of the supposedly 'unorganised' medley of market institutions it was to replace.

The third phase, which began only 10 to 15 years ago, was a re-statement in modern dress of the realism of the classical economists. It has restored the scepticism about the intentions and capacity of men in government to interpret and serve the public interest. And it is now producing a sophisticated structure of proposals for the control of government by newly-conceived economic policy and constitutional reform.

The radical development in our own lifetime has thus been no less than a fundamental, if not dramatic, change in the analysis of government. The view being replaced is that government was the solution to the deficiencies of economic and social development—in economic language, that government would repair the damage of market failure. The new view sees government itself as the cause of economic and social degeneration, both in its acts of commission and in its acts of omission. This is the intellectual divide of our times analysed by Professor Littlechild as a prelude to the succeeding papers.

. As often with IEA seminars, the audience, which comprised economists and other academics, leading commentators in the press, and men from industry, raised important present-day applications of the formal papers.

Economics of bureaucracy

With the second paper, on the economics of bureaucracy by one of its Founding Fathers, Professor Gordon Tullock of the Virginia Polytechnic Institute and State University—whose name will always be linked on this subject with that of Professor J. M. Buchanan—we enter into the latest thinking of the school on the economics of 'public choice', also known as the economics of government, democracy or politics, founded in the USA and now spreading to Europe and other continents. Professor Tullock reviewed the main elements in the new approach with special reference to the light it might shed on the reasons for the undesired growth of government.

Readers will find his graphic but simple account of the way bureaucracy works a much more satisfyingly realistic interpretation than the one that has dominated thinking in Britain (in all schools of thought and all political parties)—that bureaucrats are essentially able men who carry out the orders of politicians. There is, of course, no implied criticism of bureaucrats as men who work in public offices; but neither is there the simplistic attitude that they are better than other men in their anxiety and capacity to serve the general public in all circumstances, even when their personal interests are threatened. The notion that to make a man a public official is to make him a public benefactor is a long time a-dying.

The new economics of bureaucracy has also yielded cures for the disease of giantism. Its diagnoses and its solutions are, not surprisingly, those that have worked in the market—and they are drastic:

to promote competition within individual bureaucracies; to contract out functions, where possible, to private firms (and to competing rather than monopolistic units); to reduce salaries until voluntary resignations achieve the required reduction in size; even to withdraw the vote from bureaucrats and their families. Professor Tullock indicated these were tentative proposals, but they set thinking in new directions that seemed likely to suggest solutions more readily than the old.

The questions and discussion after Professor Tullock's paper indicated enthusiasm mingled with astonishment at the new ideas he had launched. Lord Robbins, who had known government from the inside as head of the Economic Section of the Offices of the War Cabinet from 1941 to 1945, raised some doubt about the *general* applicability of this important mode of approach. There can be be little doubt that this is a subject British economists have not hitherto developed nearly as much as they might have done. With few exceptions,[1] there are still few book-length studies of the economics of bureaucracy or of the economics of democracy in general. Perhaps the very growth of government in Britain has directed the attention of economists to methods of making government efficient, or less inefficient, rather than to the rationale of the *size* of government as it has emerged. Whatever the reasons, there has been missing that close analysis of the motivations of politicians and bureaucrats prompted by the commonsense of the classical economists and their successors—an attitude epitomised by Alfred Marshall's question: 'Do you mean Government all wise, all just, all powerful, or Government as it now is?'

Macro-economic controls

The third paper was by one of the leading analysts of the finances of government, Professor Patrick Minford. His subject was 'Macro-economic Controls on Government'. He presented an impressive and sophisticated analysis of three restrictions on governmental fiscal and monetary activities: the Budget, the money supply, and the structure of taxation and social security. He argued that the Budget should be balanced, allowing for the cyclical condition of the economy, that the money supply should grow at the rate required

---

[1] Notably *Welfare Economics: A Liberal Restatement*, by Professors C. K. Rowley and A. T. Peacock (Martin Robertson, 1975).

for the growth of real output, and that taxes and social benefits should be designed to secure a minimum income (though, for the able-bodied, below the earnings of unskilled work), the marginal tax rate should not exceed 50 per cent, and taxes should be based not on income but on expenditure. His argument provoked an animated exchange with the audience, and elicited a notable contribution from Samuel Brittan, on whose remarks Professor Minford has added a postscript. Here again Lord Robbins lent the weight of his experience in the construction of monetary and fiscal policy.

Professor Minford also discussed more briefly the macro-economic controls on government expenditure that have come into prominence more recently—cash ceilings or expenditure limits and 'planned' expenditure programmes, requiring controlled administrative procedures and forecasts of economic activity, government borrowing, etc. He properly remarked that cash limits by themselves could do nothing unless they flowed from underlying policies that reflect the political will to control government expenditure. And his conclusion was that if the political will existed, and the measures to implement it were taken, it might be unnecessary to reform the constitution in order to create new and more precise controls over the power of government to overspend.[2]

Micro-economic controls

The paper by Arthur Seldon, entitled 'Micro-Economic Controls on Government', expressed strong scepticism on the effectiveness of macro-economic controls in 'taming' inordinate government. It questioned whether these controls would be sufficient because they were operated by the same people, politicians and bureaucrats, who had inflated and distended government expenditure in the first place, and who must therefore be expected to find ways round them. Macro-economic controls, like patriotism, he argued, were not enough. The paper contended that the essence of methods to control government overspending was to put government services into the market to justify themselves by pricing in competition with any other suppliers who could provide them. Not least, micro-controls would be more certain in their effects, because they shifted the political odium from

---

[2] These constitutional questions are discussed at some length by Professor James M. Buchanan, Mr John Burton and Professor Richard Wagner in Hobart Paper 78, *The Consequences of Mr Keynes*, IEA, 1978.

the politicians, who would shy from public displeasure at 'cutting public services', and transferred it to citizen-taxpayer-consumers themselves.

Mr Seldon argued moreover that, even if government could be impelled to reduce expenditure, it would not necessarily cut where the public most preferred, since it had no machinery to discover public preferences. And the interests of politicians and bureaucrats would impel them to use a scythe that coarsely cut the flowers as well as the weeds: the services people wanted as well as those they did not.

This paper was based on the sub-division of the services supplied by government into public goods proper, for which macro-controls were the only ones available though unsatisfactory, and private benefits, which accounted for around two-thirds of current British government expenditure. The solution was therefore a structure of charging where possible over the whole range of government services. Finally, the paper briefly considered whether charging was administratively workable, socially acceptable, economically realistic, or politically possible; the obstructions to the introduction of charging; and the economic consequences of not charging.

The discussion ranged from the services for which charges might be raised—including refuse collection, medical care, slaughter-houses, education, school transport, etc.—to the measures desirable to enable people with low incomes to pay charges. These are the largely neglected issues in the control of government; their neglect is all the more mystifying since economists take in with their mother's milk the power of price to discipline demand.

Disarming the Treasury

Dr Alan Budd's paper, which followed, was a specialised but particularly authoritative examination of a central department of government, the Treasury, that illustrated one of the major propositions of the economics of bureaucracy—its power over government derived from its monopoly of the information supplied to Ministers. Dr Budd was at the Treasury from 1970 to 1974 working on medium- and short-term forecasting during the period that has begun to be called 'The Great Inflation', so his opinion carries the weight of a rare combination of knowledge and independence. He related his paper to the theme of the Seminar by what is perhaps the most fundamental criticism of recent government policy in particular and of macro-economic control of the economy in general. He contended that the Treasury had persistently promised more than it could achieve by macro-economic management, and that this gratuitous intervention in the economy entailed growing inflation and distortion. He concluded that the economic role of government should be much reduced.

His detailed criticism was that the Treasury acted as a pressure group for a particular view of how the economy worked, rather than as a secretariat to channel a diverse range of views to the Chancellor of the Exchequer. It so happens that during Dr Budd's tenure the Treasury continued its unfounded attachment to the Keynesian interpretation of history. But the more damaging conclusion is that, even if the Treasury view of the early 1970s had been right, it would still have been wrong to conceal or minimise other views: all should have had access to the Chancellor and the Cabinet. The Chancellor may have taken informal and private steps to inform himself of 'outside views', but they could not compete with the influence of the inside view of the Treasury.

Dr Budd's proposals follow from his analysis and indicate a radical change in the functions of the Treasury that it will no doubt dislike and resist. Perhaps more than anywhere else in the machinery of government, the obstruction of the Treasury will, as Professor Rowley argued later, itself have to be resisted.

The discussion again raised important implications of the paper for policy. Lord Robbins compared the British and American relationships between Ministers and their advisers, and Professor Ivor Pearce expanded on the proposal to buy in economic advice from outside sources.

Neutralising the obstructors

The final paper, by Professor Charles K. Rowley, raised perhaps the most deep-lying issues in the relationship between economic policy and the nature of British political democracy. Professor Rowley, a contributor to several recent IEA Seminars, is one of the leading British exponents of the new economics of politics. The issues he raised must have evoked disquiet about the dangers for the continuance of free institutions. He argued that, because information about the effects of government policy was imperfect, the organised pressure groups who had superior information would have more influence on government than unorganised consumers with less or no information. Government would therefore reflect the interests of the pressure groups—professional organisations, trade unions, as well as the government bureaucracy (local and national)—rather than those of individual citizens who paid for government services in taxes. The outcome was the development of corporatism in which the individual was losing the power to choose products as well as occupations. Professor Rowley then examined methods of removing the obstructions to the required reforms and the nature of the reforms themselves. He considered buying out the obstructors but argued in favour of a more fundamental solution—constitutional reforms that will prevent government from expanding beyond the wishes of the citizen. He maintained that, if these reforms fail, the alternatives will be hyperinflation, increasing state intervention with falling living standards, or the replacement of democracy by still more coercive government. Again, the discussion raised important implications of the paper and enabled Professor Rowley to elaborate his argument.

*   *   *

The papers in this *Readings* raise issues that are perhaps more far-reaching than any the Institute has published for some time. Although the theme seemed to deal with current economic policies, it goes to the roots of the British constitution and to the nature of the society that has been evolving in Britain and seems to thwart the underlying opinions and preferences of the British citizenry. It may be that the accelerated deterioration in the economy in the 1960s and in industry in the 1970s will provoke a radical reconsideration of the philosophy underlying economic policy. It may be that we are witnessing the earlier stages of such a climacteric among economists in all schools of thought and politicians in all three parties. The new Prime Minister leads a Cabinet which includes several Ministers who are apprised of the new trends in economic thinking. Mr Jo Grimond, the most considerable Liberal Party philosopher, has been writing in this kind of vein for some time. And it may be left to some of the more thoughtful Labour backbenchers, such as Mr Raymond Fletcher and Mr John Horam, to express the change in attitude their party may be adopting in the coming decade. Mr Fletcher indicated his thinking in *The Coming Confrontation*,[3] and Mr Horam

---

[3] IEA, 1978.

has advised his friends[4] that the future of his party lies with 'market socialism' which recognises that the evil has not been with private ownership but with monopoly, which can be even more objectionable in government than in the market.

The Institute is grateful to all the participants in this *Readings* and in the Seminar on which it is based, not least to Lord Robbins for presiding over it, and to Professor Gordon Tullock for coming from the USA and presenting his incisive analysis of bureaucracy in a paper that enlivened deep thinking with graphic language.

June/July 1979   ARTHUR SELDON

---

[4] *Guardian*, 4 June 1979.

Introductory Remarks

LORD ROBBINS
Seminar Chairman

The Author

LORD ROBBINS: Sometime Professor of Economics, London School of Economics and Political Science; Director of Economic Section of Offices of the War Cabinet, 1941-45. Chancellor of the University of Stirling, 1967-78. Chairman of the *Financial Times,* 1961-71. Latest works: *Political Economy Past and Present* (1977); *Against Inflation* (1979).

The title of our conference today is *The Taming of Government*. In opening the proceedings I should like to begin by emphasising that 'taming' is not to be regarded as equivalent to 'killing'. To tame a horse may make it a very useful animal; to kill it may very easily deprive you of essential services.

It is true there have been thinkers, of whom William Godwin, Shelley's father-in-law, provides the classic example, who have argued that all social evils arise from law and government and that, if they were abolished, the race might advance, to use the celebrated phrase of Malthus's polemic, 'with accelerated velocity towards illimitable and hitherto unconceived improvement'. It may sound odd, but I think it is necessary to emphasise that the arguments we are to examine today rest upon no such assumptions. It is necessary since, in current controversy, very often the arguments of classical liberalism or neo-liberalism are represented as implying the desirability of absence of law and order. How often do we hear persons who should know better, such as Mr Callaghan, fasten on their opponents the accusation of desiring an anarchy of production, a 'free for all' in economic relationships.

Liberalism requires law

Such imputations are the utter reverse of the truth. The fundamental assumption of the classical liberal conception of orderly and beneficial economic and social arrangements is the existence of law and the apparatus necessary to enforce it. The benefits of exchange and the decentralised organisation of productive activities capable of being so decentralised, rest essentially on the existence of rules and restraints which inhibit or punish anti-social behaviour. I defy any person of candour to urge the contrary; and I would also like to argue explicitly that the framework of law thus postulated does not consist of a few banal maxims capable of being written on a couple of tablets of stone. On the contrary, they are matters of very considerable length and intricacy. No one who has reflected, for example, on the complexity of the laws of property and contract can deny this obvious truth.

The classical functions of government

But beyond the highly difficult business of interpreting traditional law and adapting it to changing technical and organisational requirements, there are further functions of a centralised nature which figure large in the classical and neo-classical programme. Adam Smith defined them as follows:

'The duty of erecting and maintaining certain public works and institutions, which it can never be to the interest of any individual or small body of individuals to erect and maintain, because the profit could never repay the expense to any individual or small body of individuals, though it may frequently do much more than repay it to a great society'.

And in our own day, as has often been pointed out, John Maynard Keynes used almost the same words:

'The most important agenda of the state relates not to those activities which private individuals are already fulfilling, but to those functions which fall outside the sphere of the individual; to those decisions which are made by no-one if the state does not make them. The important thing for government is not to do things which individuals are doing already and to do them a little better or a little worse; but to do those things which at present are not done at all.'

Now this distinction made by such outstanding economists of an earlier and the present age does itself present problems of very considerable intellectual interest and political importance. What is the extent of functions which are *inevitably* only capable of central organisation? To what extent are others, so thought to be, actually capable of being performed by individuals or individual organisations. I suspect we shall touch on some of these problems today. In the present state of knowledge there is a considerable area of questions on which reasonable people may hold different opinions—the supply of money and credit, for instance, and the whole range of patent law and copyright.

—far exceeded by present-day practice

In the last hundred years, however, with vastly accelerating velocity in our own time, the activities of government have extended far beyond what Smith, or even Keynes, would have regarded as desirable.

- They have created *giant monopolies* where experience has shown that monopolistic organisation was by no means inevitable or socially beneficial.

- They have created *privileges* which mean that large sections of the community are free from legal obligations which are binding on others.
- They have imposed all sorts of *interferences with markets* which have distorted productive activity.
- They have created a persistent 'shortage' of *housing* by utterly irrational systems of rent control.
- They have spent millions keeping alive branches of industry which should have been allowed to go into liquidation, releasing capital and labour better employed elsewhere.
- They have debauched the *value of money* producing incidentally productive inefficiency and distributive injustice on a scale seldom witnessed anywhere save during wars or revolutions.

And the *philosophy* behind such developments, in so far as it has not been mere vote-catching, or other deference to vested interest, has landed us in this country in a position where the ideal of the Smith-Keynes conception of the state—restricting its activities to those which, if not done centrally will not be done at all—so far from being realised, is now stood on its head. Whether for ideological reasons—or in my judgement false conceptions of economic efficiency —existing states and their subsidiaries intrude on all sorts of functions where their performance is not only inferior to that of the decentralised activities of individuals or groups of individuals but also definitely discourages or inhibits such activities.

It is the taming of this sort of government activity, both in law and the organisation of production and distribution, which will be the main focus of our papers and the discussion that they arouse today. How can we bring it about that the activities of government are restricted to areas where their existence *promotes* rather than *impedes* the creative activities of the citizens of whose harmonious living together they are supposed to be guardians?

These are difficult questions intrinsically—and still more difficult in an historical situation in which we have progressed so dangerously far in the opposite direction and in which the reversal of so many inimical tendencies inevitably involves persuasion, ingenuity and, let us never forget—both for political and economic reasons—time to do the job properly.

It is to this subject that we have to direct our attention, and I call upon the reader of the first paper, Professor Littlechild, to address us.

1. What Should Government Do?

STEPHEN C. LITTLECHILD

University of Birmingham

The Author

STEPHEN LITTLECHILD: Professor of Commerce, University of Birmingham, since 1975. Formerly Professor of Applied Economics, University of Aston, 1973-75. Sometime Consultant to the Ministry of Transport, Treasury, World Bank, Electricity Council, American Telephone & Telegraph Co. Editor and co-author, *Operational Research for Managers,* 1977. For the IEA he wrote *The Fallacy of the Mixed Economy,* Hobart Paper 80, 1978.

I. INTRODUCTION

This paper will attempt to provide a background for the next five papers. Although it is about the work and views of economists, it is a non-technical paper written for laymen who wish to know what economists believe governments should do. But first a warning: economists today are not of one mind, nor have they ever been. Economists have not yet succeeded in establishing any definitive and universally held views *either* about the success which has attended government action in the past, *or* about the appropriate role for government in the future. No doubt an economist can be found somewhere to support almost *any* conceivable role for government.

(i) 1776-1876: classical economics

As a rough generalisation, the so-called 'classical' economists writing during the century following the publication of Adam Smith's *Wealth of Nations* (1776) favoured the development of a free-market economy [27]. The duty of the government was primarily to provide a framework of law and order within which the market could operate. Admittedly, certain other duties were identified—notably, the provision of goods and services (now known as public goods) which generate benefits to all people indiscriminately, such as defence, roads, parks, sewage disposal, etc., and the provision of education, welfare and poor relief. But these duties were not the main concern of the classical economists. Not without justification, their approach was referred to as one of *'laissez-faire'*.

(ii) 1876-1976: neo-classical 'welfare economics' and Keynesian macro-economics

During the subsequent century, from 1876 until a few years ago, we may say, as an equally rough generalisation, that economists became increasingly aware of deficiencies in the market economy, and increasingly concerned to find ways in which the government could act to overcome these. This concern eventually manifested itself in the development of so-called 'neo-classical welfare economics', on the one hand, and 'Keynesian macro-economics', on the other. A currently pervasive view amongst people in all walks of life, embodied in government policy today, is that Britain needs a 'mixed economy'

3

in which the government not merely 'holds the ring', but actively intervenes in production or to influence the production plans of others by a variety of taxes and subsidies, fiscal and financial measures, restrictions and threats. This view is a natural implication of Keynesian and welfare economics.

(iii) **1976: a return to market economics?**

In the last decade or so, there have been signs that the pendulum is swinging back again. People appear to be increasingly disillusioned with the *results* of government action. Economists are becoming increasingly sceptical about the *theoretical foundations* which Keynesian and welfare economics provide for government policies. They now doubt whether either of these theories adequately describes the ways in which (i) the market or (ii) the government work in the real world. Economists are finding that the market has hitherto-unappreciated strengths, and that government has hitherto unappreciated weaknesses. This leads, naturally, to the view that the functions of the state should once again be severely restricted—though not necessarily to the same boundary as advocated by the classical writers.

Other papers at this conference will deal with Keynesian macro-economic policy. Here, we shall outline the approach of welfare economics, the nature of the objections recently raised against it, and the kind of constitution required for government to fulfil its appropriate and limited role.

II. WELFARE ECONOMICS

Welfare economics may be seen, at least in part, as an explicit attempt to answer the question: what should government do? Distinguished British contributors to this approach include Professors A. C. Pigou [25] and J. E. Meade [20].

Much of welfare economics was based on the notion of an *efficient allocation of resources* generated by a *perfectly competitive* market, a hypothetical state of affairs in which many small firms produced a homogenous product. Since no firm was large enough to have a significant effect on supply in the market, all took the market price as given. It was assumed that all buyers and sellers in the market had perfect knowledge, in particular, that all the firms had access to exactly the same technology and resources, so all had identical costs. The possibility of free entry into the market meant that price was kept down by competition to minimum average cost. Thus, the total product was produced in the cheapest possible way, and consumers were able to choose how to spend their incomes knowing that the prices they faced correctly reflected relative marginal costs of production. Given the initial incomes of consumers, the resources of the whole economy were allocated efficiently. It was not possible to re-allocate resources so as to make everyone better off simultaneously: the only way to make someone better off was to make someone else worse off (an allocation of resources said to be 'Pareto-optimal', after the Italian economist Vilfredo Pareto (1843-1923)).

'Market failure'

It was recognised, of course, that this happy state of perfect competition did not apply throughout real-world economies. There were many cases of 'market failure', where the assumptions of perfect competition were not met.

1. *Economies of scale* may be so large compared to the size of the market that only one or a few firms are viable; so they would enjoy monopoly power, enabling them to make excess profits by setting prices above marginal cost, thereby restricting output.

2. *Externalities:* firms may not take into account some of the consequences of their actions for others; those which ignore the costs they impose on others will over-produce, or use inappropriate methods of production.

3. *Public goods,* where the cost of supply is independent of the number of recipients (e.g. TV and radio programmes,) hence prices equal to the zero *marginal* cost of supplying any service will not generate sufficient revenue to cover its *total* cost.

4. *Lack of knowledge* about the activities and plans of consumers, owners of resources and other firms, may lead to bottlenecks in production or to resources lying idle.

The existence of market failure thus means that the resources available to society are not being utilised efficiently—a 'Pareto optimum' has not been attained. In all cases it would, in principle, be possible for government to re-arrange the utilisation of resources to make *everyone* better off.

Government action to remove market failure

How could this be done in practice? The welfare economists suggested some form of government action. Control on monopoly prices seemed indicated, including the social ownership of 'natural monopolies' where competition was thought impossible. Externalities might be corrected by devising a set of taxes and subsidies. The government itself would have to produce public goods, financing them out of taxation. To deal with lack of knowledge, national planning techniques seemed to be called for, coupled with appropriate macro-economic policies for regulating demand in the economy as a whole. It was thus thought that government could ensure that the market worked *as if* it were perfectly competitive.

There was, finally, the important policy of the *distribution* of income. Nothing in the argument so far has suggested that an efficient use of resources would yield an outcome that was 'socially' desirable. It was shown, however, that *any* technically feasible outcome could be achieved by perfect competition plus an appropriate initial re-distribution of income. In this way, 'social' desirability and income distribution could be considered separately from economic efficiency.

In comparison with classical writers, the welfare economists did not so much advocate *new* activities for government as a significant extension of their *scale*. Even economists sympathetic to the classical writers acknowledge that *some* extensions of the role of government were necessary, but by no means as much as the welfare economists envisaged. For example, Professor Robbins, while denying that size of firm *per se* is an index of monopoly power, accepts the need for some form of intervention to prevent collusion. Contrast, however, the Robbins view that

'We should not be too fussy when some probably transitory monopoly emerges' [27, p. 58],

with Professor J. E. Meade's concern that

'There is a horrifying tendency in our present society to allow, indeed to encourage, the formation of huge monopolistic concentrations of power which are not necessary on technical grounds and which are subject to a minimum of social control. Giant industrial concerns may be formed and achieve great market power and undue political influence, even though the technical production advantages of unified control on so gigantic a scale are not very great.' [20, p. 46]

Or again, Professor Robbins's view that
'the invisible hand has to move within limits which preclude gross diseconomies'
(i.e. externalities [27, p. 39]) is a far cry from Professor Meade's proposition that
'the authorities should make a grand tour around the whole economy taxing those activities which are socially costly according to the degree of social costs which they involve.' [20, p. 113]

III. THE GROWING SCEPTICISM OF WELFARE ECONOMICS

The recent attack on welfare economics has come on two fronts: its representation of market behaviour and government behaviour.

Many economists, such as Joan Robinson [28] of Cambridge and E. H. Chamberlin [5] of Harvard in the 1930s, challenged the reality of perfect competition, but replaced it by other concepts such as imperfect or monopolistic competition which were equally *static* and obsessed with the equilibrium state. Adam Smith and his immediate successors thought of competition quite differently. For them, competition was a continuing and *dynamic* process of adjustment, in which each firm tries to outdo its rivals, by offering a better price or quality of product, instead of the same product at the same price [21, 22].

This idea has been developed in recent years by members of the so-called Austrian school of economics, notably Mises [23], Hayek [14] and Kirzner [17]. They have emphasised the lack of knowledge in the economy, and the role of competition as a discovery process and as a device for co-ordinating the plans of millions of consumers, producers and resource owners largely unknown to each other.

Similar ideas have been developed by Richardson [26], Shackle [29] and Wiseman [31] in Britain, and by Brozen [1] and Demsetz [11] in the USA.[1] The general implication of their arguments is that the market economy cannot be judged as though it worked in a world of perfect knowledge. The merits of competition lie precisely in its ability to handle *imperfect* knowledge. Actions and institutions which seem inefficient in a perfect world may be quite efficient in the real imperfect one in which we live.

---

[1] Also Littlechild [18].

'Government failure'

The second front of the attack on welfare economics concerns the behaviour of government. Will a government organisation in the real world step in to correct market failure? If there is market failure, can there not be 'government failure'? Should we not develop an explanation of how government *does* behave, rather than how it *should* behave?

Major contributors to this line of thought include the public choice theorists Buchanan and Tullock [4] from Virginia; the proponents of an economic theory of regulation, notably Stigler [30] and Posner [24] from Chicago; and those who have developed the economics of property rights, notably Coase [6] of Chicago and Demsetz [10] of UCLA. Among British economists there are Wiseman, Rowley and Peacock [3].

These economists emphasise the nature of the choice facing the decision-maker in public life, whether cabinet minister, politician, civil servant, local government officer or manager in a nationalised industry. His actions will emerge in the light of his own evaluation of their consequences, particularly those which affect him personally. It cannot be assumed that his sole mission in life is objectively to detect and remedy cases of 'market failure'.

IV. GOVERNMENT, MONOPOLY AND MARKET EFFICIENCY

There are four main types of government organisation designed to counteract monopoly and ensure efficiency in the market [18].

(1) The Monopolies and Mergers Commission may be asked to investigate activities likely to operate against the public interest. The Price Commission vets the price increases of large firms. In both, the cause for concern is high or 'excessive' profit, which is thought to reflect monopoly power. Not only is this profit thought to be at the expense of the consumer, but it is thought that society as a whole suffers from the consequent restriction of output. Moreover, it is recently being suggested that large firms have earned excessive profits but are forced to dissipate them in wasteful competition to attain monopoly positions [9].

If competition is seen as a dynamic process, however, such profits will appear as the result of superior alertness or ability. They are not earned at the expense of consumers; on the contrary, they are a sign that customers have been provided with a better product than was otherwise available to them. This success will, in turn, stimulate other firms to respond or surpass the original profit-maker. On the contrary, government policy designed to prevent the emergence of profits will, *ipso facto*, discourage the discovery of new and better products and techniques of production.

(2) The National Enterprise Board is required to identify pockets of inefficiency in the economy and remedy them, either by buying up and revitalising firms or by restructuring whole industries. Many such centres of inefficiency undoubtedly exist. But why has the market not rooted them out?

The truth is that the market does not know where they are. Certainly one may identify firms and industries losing money and laying off workers. But do they have a future if properly managed, or are they best left to contract? If the future were known, the answer would be available. Since it is not known, is there any reason why the NEB should be more able and willing to discern it than the owners and managers of private capital? Is the NEB not more concerned to be seen 'doing something', especially solving the unemployment problem, than to identify what, in the long run, will be the most efficient use of the country's scarce resources?

(3) Welfare economists tend to think of nationalisation as a cure for natural monopoly. Following their advice, the government has instructed nationalised industries to behave 'as if' they were perfectly competitive, by setting prices equal to marginal costs and appraising investments according to a test discount rate or required rate of return [7, 8]. This framework of control has proved totally unsuccessful. Why?

First, it assumes that the products and technologies are 'given'; it fails to provide any incentive to the industry to discover new and better approaches. It is thus a static framework out of place in the dynamic world. Second, it assumes that both industries and sponsoring government departments wish *above all* to achieve efficient resource allocation, when plainly they wish nothing of the sort. Managers, civil servants and politicians have their own objectives, which may include protecting their industry, avoiding bad publicity and achieving the smooth (rather than efficient) running of the industries under their control. Instructions on marginal cost pricing

9

and investment appraisal are at best irrelevant, and at worst a nuisance, in furthering these objectives [31].

(4) To curb the power of natural monopolies to inflate prices, the United States has tended to *regulate* industries rather than nationalise them. In the event, as empirical work has shown, there has been virtually no difference between the pricing policies of regulated and unregulated electricity utilities. The Bell Telephone System appears to charge monopoly prices on its interstate routes despite federal regulation [19]. This ineffectiveness of regulation has led some critics to suggest that the regulatory commissions are eventually 'captured' by the industries they purport to regulate [30]. More generally, it is suggested that government regulation of many different kinds is designed and operated in response to the interests of powerful employee pressure groups, rather than with the consumer and efficient resource allocation in mind [24]. These theories of economic regulation enable us better to appreciate the political pressures behind the practice of nationalisation, and the futility of expecting a policy of marginal cost pricing to have a significant effect.

Many economists are thus beginning to doubt whether government has a useful role to play in countering monopoly or inefficiency by active interventionist agencies. Such agencies invariably come, on the contrary, to *limit* competition and protect vested interests. Unfettered competition from existing or potential rivals is likely to be more effective and less partisan in avoiding the dangers of monopoly and inefficiency.

V. GOVERNMENT AND THE ENVIRONMENT

There is growing concern that economic growth is leading to a decline in the quality of the environment, and increasing pressure on the government to 'do something'. The layman's instinctive suggestion is for some form of direct control over resources, especially prohibition on their excessive use—for example, exclusive bus lanes to discourage private cars and thereby alleviate road congestion; limitations on the number of aircraft landings, especially at night, to reduce noise and nuisance; quotas to prevent over-exploitation of fisheries.

Welfare economists identified these effects as externalities: people using the resources had no incentive to take into account the consequences of their actions for others, so there was excessive usage. The remedy proposed was not explicit and detailed regulation, which would most likely be too inflexible. Instead, a system of taxes and subsidies was proposed, equal to the external costs (or benefits), so that each user was led to take account of the consequences for others.

To my knowledge this idea has been applied only once. In Singapore, a 'congestion tax' has been imposed on morning rush-hour traffic entering the city. Apparently, the scheme has been a big success with all concerned, since congestion has been virtually eliminated and the government enjoys an additional income. In Britain, the Civil Aviation Authority has recently proposed a 'noise tax' on aircraft movements, which has a similar rationale.

Economists now recognise that taxes and subsidies are not the only solution to externalities. Indeed, they may be a far from adequate solution. They require much information to compute. They may be as inflexible as regulations in responding to changes in the environment. They may even provide incorrect incentives—airlines may be led to install sound-reducing devices which are more expensive than the cost of double-glazing and sound-proofing houses. Finally, the virtual absence of externality taxes and subsidies testifies to the effective political resistance to their use.

It was the crucial contribution of Professor Ronald Coase to show the relationship between externalities and *property rights* [6]. If it were possible costlessly to negotiate with the potentially injured parties, externalities would not exist, and there would be no misallocation of resources. This diagnosis suggests that an alternative approach to environmental problems would be to define and enforce private property rights in the affected resources. Indeed it has been suggested that private property rights developed in the past precisely as an efficient social response to externalities [10]. Householders might be given private 'noise rights' above their property, which airlines would have to purchase (at a fee acceptable to the householder) if they wished to fly overhead. Private fishing rights in the North Sea might be defined and auctioned off, so that each owner would have an incentive to conserve his fish. In effect, what is proposed here is an 'enclosure movement' of the air and sea, analogous to the land enclosure movement of the 18th century, which would enable parcels of air and sea to be traded on private markets just as land is now.

Here, then, is an active and important role for government: defining and enforcing new property rights so as to aid the smooth functioning of the economy. It is, of course, merely an aspect of the government's duty to provide a framework of law and order, but if this duty were properly and intelligently fulfilled, it would obviate the need for many planning regulations, commissions of inquiry and other government agencies.

VI. GOVERNMENT AND THE CONSTITUTION

During the past century, economists gradually came to see government as a means of improving the workings of the market economy and alleviating its supposed defects. During the past decade, however, there has been increasing scepticism about this view. The massive growth of government in post-war years has self-evidently *not* solved Britain's problems, but rather exacerbated them. *Government is more and more seen as the protector of powerful vested interests rather than the promoter of efficiency for the benefit of the country as a whole.* It is increasingly recognised that prosperity and freedom in Britain depend crucially upon the survival of the market economy, which must be protected *from* government if it is to survive.

Economists and political scientists like Hayek [15, 16a, 16b], Buchanan [2] and Ferns [12] have thus been led to examine the problems posed by democracy.[1] If government must respond to short-term electoral pressures, it will be unable to take the long-run view in the interests of the country as a whole. Events in Britain daily confirm this argument. It is necessary, therefore, to design a constitution to *protect government against special interest groups.* This might be done by more clearly separating the legislative (law-making) function of Parliament from its executive (day-to-day government) function. The legislature would comprise democratically elected members, only a proportion of whom would be elected each year, with each member holding office for a long period, thereby avoiding the need to respond to party or political pressures. Such a legislature would impose a tighter framework within which the executive government would necessarily operate.

---

[1] See also Hailsham [13].

VII. CONCLUSIONS

Whereas the classical economists envisaged a minimal role for the government, essentially providing a framework within which the market economy could operate, welfare economists have developed a theoretical approach which implies, in practice, an all-pervasive role for government in the economy. Not only should it provide law and order, defence and roads, relief of sickness and unemployment; it should also regulate or nationalise large firms, tax or subsidise socially costly or desirable activities, and co-ordinate or plan the future development of the economy. These theoretical arguments, coupled with political expediency, have led to a massive extension in the scope and volume of government activities. Britain has suffered as a result.

During the last decade, economists have increasingly come to recognise that welfare economics fails to embody an accurate perception of the workings of either the market or the government. Newer analyses, theories or diagnoses which take account of ignorance and alertness, and the personal and political pressures impinging upon all decisions, reach very different conclusions. The appropriate role of government is once more strictly limited to providing a suitable legal and institutional framework for the market, but now there is a recognition that this framework must constantly be developed and revised. It is, moreover, of paramount importance to protect the government from short-term electoral pressures to do otherwise. A revised constitution is thus seen as necessary to protect the country from an unwarranted and undesirable extension in the role of government.

REFERENCES

[1] Brozen, Y., 'Bain's Concentration and Rates of Return Revisited', *J. Law & Economics,* Vol. XIV, No. 2, October 1971.

[2] Buchanan, J. M., *The Limits of Liberty: Between Anarchy and Leviathan,* Chicago: University of Chicago Press, 1975.

[3] Buchanan, J. M. *et al., The Economics of Politics,* London: IEA Readings 18, 1978.

[4] Buchanan, J. M., and Tullock, G., *The Calculus of Consent,* University of Michigan Press, Ann Arbor, 1962.

[5] Chamberlin, Edward H., *The Theory of Monopolistic Competition*, Cambridge: Harvard Univ. Press, 1933, 8th edn., 1965.

[6] Coase, R. H., 'The Problem of Social Cost', *J. Law & Econs.*, Vol. 3, 1960, pp. 1-44.

[7] Cmnd. 3437, *Nationalised Industries: A Review of Economic and Social Objectives*, London: HMSO, 1967.

[8] Cmnd. 7131, *The Nationalised Industries*, London: HMSO, March 1978.

[9] Cowling, K. & Mueller, D. C., 'The Social Costs of Monopoly Power', *Economic Journal*, Volume 88, pp. 727-48, December 1978.

[10] Demsetz, H., 'Towards a Theory of Property Rights', *American Economic Review*, (Proceedings), Vol. 57, May 1967, pp. 347-359.

[11] Demsetz, H., 'Information and Efficiency: Another Viewpoint', *Journal of Law and Economics*, Vol. XII, No. 1, April 1969, pp. 1-22.

[12] Ferns, H. S., *The Disease of Government*, Temple Smith, 1978.

[13] Hailsham, Lord, *The Dilemma of Democracy: Diagnosis and Prescription*, London: Collins, 1978.

[14] Hayek, F. A., *Individualism and Economic Order*, Chicago: University Press, 1948.

[15] Hayek, F. A., *Economic Freedom and Representative Government*, Occasional Paper 39, London: IEA, 1973.

[16] Hayek, F. A., *Law, Legislation and Liberty*, Routledge and Kegan Paul, (a) Vol. 1, *Rules and Order*, 1973; (b) Vol. 2, *The Mirage of Social Justice*, 1976.

[17] Kirzner, I. M., *Competition and Entrepreneurship*, Chicago: University of Chicago Press, 1973.

[18] Littlechild, S. C., *The Fallacy of the Mixed Economy*, Hobart Paper No. 80, London: IEA, June 1978.

[19] Littlechild, S. C., & Rousseau, J. J., 'Pricing Policy of a US Telephone Company', *Journal of Public Economics*, Vol. 4, 1975, pp. 35-56.

[20] Meade, J. E., *The Intelligent Radical's Guide to Economic Policy: The Mixed Economy*, London: George Allen & Unwin, 1975.

[21] McNulty, P. J., 'A Note on the History of Perfect Competition', *Journal of Political Economy*, Vol. 75, Aug. 1967.

[22] McNulty, P. J., 'The Meaning of Competition', *Quarterly Journal of Economics,* Vol. 82, Nov. 1968, pp. 639-56.

[23] Mises, L., von, *Human Action,* Chicago: Henry Regnery Co., 1st edn., 1949, 3rd rev. edn., 1963.

[24] Posner, R. A., 'Taxation by Regulation', *Bell Journal of Economics & Management Science,* Vol. 2, No. 1, Spring 1971, pp. 22-50.

[25] Pigou, A. C., *The Economics of Welfare,* Macmillan, London, 1912, 4th edn., 1920.

[26] Richardson, G. B., *Information and Investment,* Oxford: Oxford University Press, 1960.

[27] Robbins, L., *Political Economy Past and Present,* Macmillan, 1976.

[28] Robinson, Joan, *The Economics of Imperfect Competition,* London, 1933.

[29] Shackle, G. L. S., *Epistemics and Economics,* Cambridge: Cambridge University Press, 1972.

[30] Stigler, G. J., 'The Theory of Economic Regulation', *Bell Journal of Economics & Management Science,* Vol. 2, No. 1, Spring 1971.

[31] Wiseman, J., 'The Political Economy of Nationalised Industry', in J. M. Buchanan *et al., The Economics of Politics,* IEA Readings 18, London, 1978.

Questions and Discussion

LAWRENCE ORCHARD (*Ever Ready*): Lord Robbins, both you and Professor Littlechild made general reference to the functions of central government, defence, law and order, the supply of services which could not otherwise be carried out by private enterprise. I may be anticipating the programme later in the day, but I would be interested to hear both your and Professor Littlechild's views on the responsibility, possibly the rights, of government in the issue of money. We have had a succession of Chancellors of the Exchequer over the last 40 years who have been both forgers because they print money and thieves because they thereby depreciate its value. What are your views on the curtailment of government power in the printing of money?

LORD ROBBINS: I will leave the answer to that question to Professor Littlechild, only stating that I certainly think the question falls into that

15

area of discussion which I indicated in my opening remarks where reasonable people can easily take two views. It is very clear that historically metal has done better than paper, but it is not at all clear either how metal should be controlled once you have a credit system, and certainly there is no consensus among professional economists, who otherwise might take different views on matters of politics, on the management of credit and money. Having said that, I pass the buck to Professor Littlechild.

PROF. LITTLECHILD: I ought to pass it back again, because, as I said, my paper was explicitly devoted to welfare economics. I will pass it to later speakers on macro-economics.

LORD ROBBINS: May I add that I think you are perhaps a little unkind to Keynes in bracketing him with neo-Keynesians. Keynes was not only anti-deflationary at the time of the most colossal deflation by the Federal Reserve Board in the United States, which certainly was responsible, in part at any rate, for the depth of the 'Thirties depression. He also stood —and it is unjust not to credit him with this—for the avoidance of inflation. The last book he published, *How to Pay for the War*, was a disquisition on how to run the war without more inflation than was absolutely inevitable. I personally regard the death of Keynes as one of the great economic disasters. He was one of the few people who could have frightened Ministers into pursuing more sensible policies than they have pursued in the last 30 years.

GORDON RICHARDS (*Hammersmith & West London College of Further Education*): Presumably government would have to be protected by constitutionally entrenched clauses to protect it from political pressures.

PROF. LITTLECHILD: I do not pretend to be an expert on these proposals. They were thrown in towards the end of my talk as an indication of the unfamiliar areas to which economists have been led. What I would believe to be the case is that a legislative body such as I suggested, elected in the way described, would be able to lay down conditions, for example, that the budget must always be balanced so that the day-to-day government, though it might like to run an inflationary budget for electoral reasons, would not be able to do so.

LORD ROBBINS: There are two thought-provoking works on this subject: Lord Hailsham's book on democracy[1] which makes extremely good reading, and the third volume of Hayek's book on *Law, Legislation*

---

[1] *The Dilemma of Democracy*, Collins, 1978.

and Liberty,[2] in which he propounds an entirely new set of constitutional arrangements. I wonder whether Professor Littlechild had that in mind?

PROF. LITTLECHILD: Certainly it was the first two volumes of his work and his indications on the third volume that I had in mind. I might mention also my colleague Professor Harry Ferns's book, *The Disease of Government,*[3] which comes to very similar conclusions. Then there is Professor J. M. Buchanan from Virginia, whose book *The Limits of Liberty: Between Anarchy and Leviathan*[4] contains similar ideas.

DR RALPH HORWITZ (*London Regional Management Centre*): While being entirely sympathetic to your position, Professor Littlechild, it does often seem to me that this critique does not handle the problem in what one might describe as the Pavlovian dog response. One does not know whether the dog is salivating because of incentive or anxiety. I think that almost everybody has a kind of floating exchange rate between their anxieties and their ambitions. I suggest that the problem of government is that individuals, and I suspect this includes university academics as well, frequently have a particular position on the floating exchange rate in which they look to government for some action or other, and at other times they hope that government will just go away. I am familiar with Professor Hayek's new thesis, but I am not entirely persuaded that it really comes to grips with this problem.

PROF. LITTLECHILD: I think economists have not studied it in quite that way, but certainly you could say that people feel that some things ought to be done by government, for example, or that we ought to do some things collectively rather than alone or within private organisations. People might give to charity, for example, providing everybody else does so. A decision by Britain to give to countries abroad would therefore be the kind of policy they would like. I do not think economists have had much to say about that kind of problem. I agree it is the kind of thing that ought to be grappled with and that has not been tackled satisfactorily by welfare economics.

RONALD HALSTEAD (*Beecham Group*): There is a practical matter coming up fairly soon in relation to your comments on the Price Commission and the Monopolies Commission. There are suggestions that they should be merged, that perhaps the Price Commission should be abolished and there should be a more effective Monopolies Commission. Have you any advice to give to government?

---

[2] Maurice Temple Smith, 1978.

[3] *The Political Order of a Free People,* Routledge & Kegan Paul, 1979.

[4] University of Chicago Press, Chicago, 1975.

PROF. LITTLECHILD: I think the first task is to abolish the Price Commission—I can see no justification for it. I quite like the Monopolies Commission because, in its early days, at least, people like Professor G. C. Allen were critical of welfare economics; he tended to take a view which was in sympathy with the view I have taken here that competition is a process. He was much more concerned that there should be an opportunity for other firms to compete. Thus, for example, he would be critical of practices which prevented entry by competitors. And that might of course include patents. On the other hand he was not critical of the large firm *per se*. So I think I would advise the Government to abolish the Price Commission and leave the Monopolies Commission as a device for securing information about practices that may tend to restrict competition. And possibly mergers, though I am not sure we really need to worry too much about mergers. I think those would be my main recommendations.

LORD ROBBINS: May I put a question from the chair? I was a little relieved to hear your qualified commendation of the Monopolies Commission. It was certainly devised by economists who to some extent shared your outlook: Professor John Jewkes, for instance, had a good deal to do with devising the original proposals for the Monopolies Commission.

But it is not clear to me that all legislation in this respect is necessarily doomed to disaster. The literature of monopoly and anti-monopoly legislation in the United States is so enormous that one cannot quote any authoritative consensus. But I have the impression, drawn from perhaps a limited reading, that if there had been nothing like the Sherman Act there would have been a good deal more monopoly of a rather intractable kind knocking about the United States. It is not clear to me that the Sherman Act, with all its complications which make that branch of public life in the United States a lawyer's paradise, can be written off as an entire failure.

PROF. LITTLECHILD: It is certainly one of the subjects where reasonable men can disagree. I am not so sure why you say 'intractable monopoly'. If we had no restrictions on mergers in this country a significantly higher number of mergers might go through, but whether they would prove to be intractable, i.e. whether the companies so formed would be able to persist as monopolies in the face of competition, is not clear. And if they did, is this not to be approved? Is this not a sign that they are more efficient?

LORD ROBBINS: With advancing technology you have to take account of the complications of the law regarding patents and licences of right, where there is certainly some incentive to form combinations which do not necessarily, without invoking all the metaphysics of welfare economics, tend to satisfy what might be assumed to have been the requirements of Adam Smith, not to mention later writers.

PROF. LITTLECHILD: That is true. But I think patents are significant only in a small proportion of British industry. There are large firms which seem to be equally dangerous to society in industries where patents are not significant. Secondly, if it is patents that are the problem, it seems to me that we ought to tackle them directly, possibly by reducing the duration of patents or even abolishing them in some spheres.

LORD ROBBINS: I am not against the law relating to patents. My dear departed friend Arnold Plant sometimes suggested total scepticism in that respect. It is a very difficult matter. As regards monopolistic collusion, it is clear that collaring a lot of patents for which there is no efficient substitute is one of the incentives.

PROF. LITTLECHILD: I agree.

PROF. GORDON TULLOCK (*Virginia Polytechnic & State University*): What of tariffs as a protection against competition? Should they not be reviewed? Senator Sherman was a great believer in high tariffs, and in a way he was remedying a problem that he had himself created.

PROF. LITTLECHILD: This of course was the suggestion put forward by the Monopolies Commission in the case of colour film. The difficulty was that the Government said it could not possibly remove the tariff (because of international trade agreements), but that would have been a way to solve the problem.

2. Bureaucracy and the Growth of Government

GORDON TULLOCK

Center for Study of Public Choice,
Virginia Polytechnic Institute
& State University

The Author

GORDON TULLOCK is University Distinguished Professor of Economics and Public Choice, Virginia Polytechnic Institute and State University. Universities of South Carolina, 1959-62, Virginia, 1962-67, and Rice, 1967-78. Editor of *Public Choice*. Co-author with Professor James M. Buchanan of *The Calculus of Consent* (1962). Author of *The Politics of Bureaucracy* (1965); *Private Wants, Public Means* (1970); *The Vote Motive* (Hobart Paperback 9, IEA, 1976, second impression 1978); 'The Charity of the Uncharitable', in *The Economics of Charity* (IEA Readings 12, 1974).

Introducing Professor Tullock, Lord Robbins said:

Our speakers have already been described, as usual, by that very efficient private enterprise, the Institute of Economic Affairs, in a page of potted biographies. But you would wish me to extend a very special welcome to Professor Tullock, who has come all this way, travelling through the night, prepared to come into action no sooner than he arrives. It is the first time that I have had the opportunity of meeting Professor Tullock, although I have long admired his work.

I. BUREAUCRACY AND GOVERNMENT

The title 'Bureaucracy and the Growth of Government' may seem redundant. For most people the outstanding characteristic of government growth is simply that bureaucracy grows and becomes more omnipresent. The purpose of this paper is to discuss the role of bureaucracy in prompting the growth of government. Bureaucracy is not only a *product* of large government; it is one of its *causal* factors. Indeed, there may be a cyclical process in which the power of the bureaucracy leads to a growth of government which in turn enlarges the size of bureaucracy and hence its power with the result that there is a further growth of government.[1]

Cause and result of big government

Obviously I am not claiming that bureaucracy is the sole or even the most important cause of the growth of government, merely that it is one of the causes as well as one of the results. That it can be one of the causes should surprise no one. Bureaucracy after all is powerful, and there are gains to bureaucrats from the expansion of the government. That they would use their power to obtain these goals seems obvious.

This assertion will no doubt shock a number of people. Government employees are frequently alleged to be primarily interested in seeking out some abstract entity called 'the public good'. Another theory which is very popular in England is that they simply implement basic

---

[1] My 'Dynamic Bureaucracy Hypothesis', *Public Choice*, No. 19, Fall 1974, pp. 127-31, amplifies this general argument.

23

policy decisions made by elected officials. Bureaucrats in England generally refer to the politicians at the very top of each department or bureau as 'our masters'. This attitude at least implies that the bureaucrats themselves have little power over those 'masters' who make all the basic decisions which the bureaucrats simply carry out.

Bureaucrats, and for that matter their political 'masters', are much like other men. There are among them scoundrels and saints, but both are rare. The average bureaucrat or politician is not markedly different from the average business man or college professor.[2] They are, like the rest of us, to some extent interested in the public good and in helping their fellow men; but, like the rest of us, they put far more time and attention into their private concerns. Thus the bureaucrat, in making a decision about some matter, is likely to give more weight to the effect of his decision on his personal career than on the nation as a whole. These two categories are not, of course, necessarily in conflict, but sometimes they are. And then we must expect the bureaucrat most of the time to choose his personal well-being rather than the public good.

These common human characteristics affect the bureaucrat's behaviour. First, bureaucrats, as you and I, are more interested in their own career and family prospects than in the public good. Secondly, in addition to the pay or perquisites that go with their jobs, they presumably like the power as well. This is a characteristic in which bureaucrats have somewhat more opportunity to indulge their preferences than the average citizen. The government, after all, is a coercive apparatus; it compels obedience. Industry and commerce are not; business men must attract customers in a competitive market.

Business men and bureaucrats

In one area however, some business men probably have more power than civil servants. The business men dealing with the employees of their firm may well (depending on the specific arrangements with the trade unions) have more control over them than a high-level bureaucrat has over low-level bureaucrats. It is extremely hard either to fire or demote a bureaucrat and less difficult for business to get rid of employees. Hence a business man (unions permitting) may be able to control his subordinates better than a bureaucrat can control

---

[2] Many college professors, including me, are government employees, and hence presumably should be listed as bureaucrats.

his bureaucratic subordinates, and certainly better than the political 'masters' can control the bureaucracy as a whole.

Thus, internal discipline and control would be better in businesses than in bureaucracies, but the ability of bureaucracy and indeed individual bureaucracies to exercise coercion on people who are not members of their own organisation is very much stronger than the ability of a business man in a like case. Some years ago the *Economist* ran a 'manifesto for a new party'. One of the planks was to bring vital ('basic') industries, such as coal, railways, airlines under popular control; it therefore proposed they immediately be converted into private corporations.

Democratic controls on bureaucracy weak

The ability of bureaucrats to avoid compliance with orders from above in pursuance of their duties means that 'democratic' controls over them are correspondingly weak. It is certainly quite possible that General Motors pays much more attention to the preferences and desires of the average American than does British Leyland to the preferences and desires of the average Englishman. This is not because the board of directors of General Motors is more concerned with pleasing its customers than is the British cabinet with pleasing the voter, but because it has much more control over the lower-level officials who actually make the decisions than the cabinet of Britain has over the lower-level officials with roughly corresponding duties.

Finally, a characteristic of bureaucrats, which they are in a uniquely strong position to fulfil, is that they like to carry out their own ideas of what is right, just and proper. Once again they are no different from you and me, but they are much more able to stick to their guns than would a man in private industry. If I have a policy I think good, I can probably keep at it for a long time as a bureaucrat even if I am the only person in the world who thinks it good. If I have a car design I think good, and I am the only person in the world who thinks it a good car, I can no doubt drive a car of that design myself but I will not be able to inflict my preferences on other people.

II. BUREAUCRACY POWER AND POLICY

The main purpose of this paper is to discuss the role of bureaucrats in expanding government. So far I have discussed their role in the government, i.e. an indication of their kind of power. This is, how-

25

ever, very important for the ability to influence policy in the direction of bureaucratic expansion. In the United States from the reign of Andrew Jackson until the beginning and then rapid expansion of the 'merit system' at the end of the 19th and the beginning of the 20th century, all Federal government employees held jobs at the pleasure of their political superiors, and in practice the bulk of them were fired every time the party in control of the government changed. This system is far from ideal, but it meant that the average civil servant was not in a position to bring significant pressure to bear upon his elected superiors because they could always fire him.

With the development of security of tenure for civil servants, this position has changed. Indeed, the American civil service was small and had no real tendency to grow before this 'reform'. It is now much safer for civil servants to defy their 'masters'; in particular through their votes they have at least potential power to fire the elected politicians who are their nominal masters. In substantially every modern democratic state, the civil service together with their families are much more numerous than the difference in votes between the contesting parties. Normally, of course, they do not cast a block vote, but if one of the parties severely annoyed the civil servants it would certainly greatly impair its electoral chances. Politicians know this and normally avoid this kind of activity.[3]

Civil servants' opposition to tax cutting

Proposals to reduce the costs of local government have been put directly to United States voters. Voting statistics in the USA are available by precinct, and we also have a fair idea of the type of people who live in each precinct. These figures make it possible through statistical means to get a good idea of how various groups of the population vote. Uniformly, *civil servants are less in favour of reduction in government expenditures; in most cases they are more strongly opposed to it than the population as a whole.*

We must be careful here not to exaggerate the size of this phenomenon. In California, for example, it would appear that the civil servants were very nearly equally divided on 'Proposition 13'. The electorate which limited the powers of the government, however,

---

[3] [Such a conflict seemed to arise between the teachers' unions and the Minister for Education, then Mrs Shirley Williams, several days before the 1979 General Election.—ED.]

was about two-thirds in favour. If we eliminate various pensioner groups, such as people on relief, etc., who pay practically no taxes, the remainder of the population would have been even more strongly in favour of Proposition 13.[4]

Further, this was a rather special case. The state was known to have a budgetary surplus of $5 billion which the governor proposed to spend on building a satellite for the state of California. Most of the civil servants could feel fairly confident that this money was available to cushion the blow.

In other states where similar votes have occurred and similar research projects have been undertaken, the same picture emerges. Civil servants are not unanimously opposed to these restrictions on taxes, but they show much stronger antagonism to them than does the population as a whole. Once again we should not be surprised. Further, the fact that they are not overwhelmingly opposed comes very largely from the phenomenon mentioned above, i.e. that politicians know of the civil servants' power. In all of these cases detailed provisions to minimise the impact of the proposed tax reduction on the civil servants have been included. The politicians favouring these restrictions do not want to take on the Civil Service directly and openly.

Nevertheless, where such referenda have failed, civil servants very generally provide the necessary marginal votes. A direct proposal to cut government expenditures by, say, simply lowering the pay of civil servants (and there is a lot of room for that, as I will show below) would be regarded by most people as 'politically impossible'.

Once again we should not be particularly surprised. The civil servants, like the rest of us, tend to vote in terms of their own interest. It happens, however, that their interest is intimately connected with certain government policies. In general they will gain from increases in the size of government and lose from its reduction. They would also, of course, like to have higher wages. There is no doubt that these factors have been important in the growth of government, although we have not been able to measure their exact weight.

In general, the voting power of the civil servants does not take the form of well-organised groups promising to swing votes of their

---

[4] [A report of a poll on a British 'Proposition 13', and comparisons with the California vote, are in Chapter 2 of *Over-Ruled on Welfare*, Hobart Paperback 13, IEA 1979.—ED.]

members for the party that offers them the most expansion, etc. There are some civil service unions in the United States, and presumably in Britain, who talk in this way, but I think it is basically a minor phenomenon. The real situation is simply that a politician who wants to get elected realises he has to take a position not regarded by the mass of civil servants as 'anti-civil service'. There are many apparently attractive political positions which would benefit the general public but harm civil servants (below). Politicians have been notably reluctant to adopt such positions, and presumably the reason is fear of pushing this very large group of voters into their opponent's camp. The net result has been a gradual expansion and improvement of the conditions of civil servants, which undeniably contributes to the growth of government.

III. BUREAUCRATS AND THE DEMAND FOR BUREAUCRACY

Bureaucratic lobbying

Bureaucrats also expand the size of government by lobbying on their own behalf since they are right inside the government policy-forming organs. They frequently have what amounts to a monopoly or near-monopoly of technical information about government policies, with the result that their advice will be the only technically competent advice that the government receives. And in carrying out their own duties they may be able to manipulate the details of policy so as to increase the demand for, and the rewards paid to, bureaucrats. All of these powers can be used to expand the size of bureaucracy. Further, they interact with the bureaucratic voting power and one another.

Why is it possible for bureaucrats to produce more than is really wanted? A model now quite well known in the economics of bureaucracy[5] is shown in Figure 1. Public services which can be produced at a constant price are shown by the horizontal line. All

---

[5] For a more comprehensive but still basically elementary discussion see my *The Vote Motive*, with a British commentary by Morris Perlman, Hobart Paperback No. 9, IEA, 1976. Further elaboration of this model is in William A. Niskanen, *Bureaucracy and Representative Government,* Aldine, Atherton, Chicago and New York, 1971 (reworked in compressed form in *Bureaucracy: Servant or Master?*, Hobart Paperback No. 5, IEA, 1973), or my own *The Politics of Bureaucracy,* Public Affairs Press, Washington, DC, 1976.

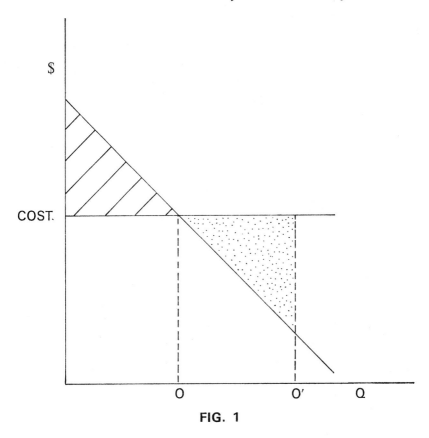

FIG. 1

demand curves slant downwards to the right, which simply means that we are willing to pay less for the 100,000th unit of something than we were for the first. There are very peculiar exceptions to this rule, but as a generalisation it seems to apply to substantially everything.

In a well-functioning competitive market the consumers, in this case the government, would purchase the service up to the point where the demand curve crossed the cost line, i.e. quantity 0. They would pay a total price for it equivalent to the rectangle to the left of line 0, and receive a net benefit from the provision of the service equal to the shaded triangle above and to the left. Private monopoly, of course, could extort part of that triangle out of the consumer, but a government monopoly is a somewhat different proposition.

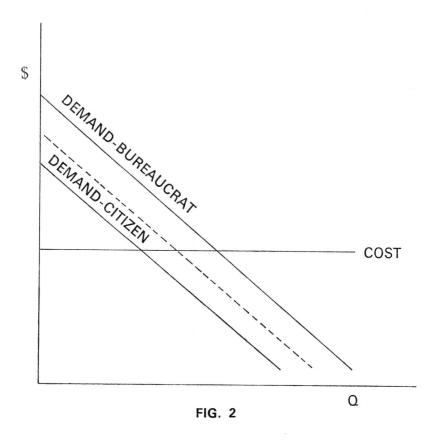

FIG. 2

Let us assume that the bureaucrats who run a government bureau cannot simply take any monopoly profit home with them. They will, however, benefit in various ways if their bureau is expanded. Further, they 'sell' their services to the government on an annual basis for whatever is their budget appropriation. In these circumstances they can theoretically expand the size of the government bureau out to 0′. At 0′ the benefit the citizenry gets from the shaded triangle is used to pay the cost, which is higher than the government's demand, and is shown by the dotted triangle.

The diagram shows perfect adjustment, i.e. bureaucrats have exploited all the gain there is to be made, and it does not therefore seem very realistic (below). Consider the situation. The government is buying more of the quantity than it wants at the price, but granted a choice between buying 0′ at the cost shown or getting nothing it will choose to buy 0′. What it would prefer, of course, is a smaller quantity of the good at that price, but if bureaucrats can convince the government that this alternative does not exist, and they are very good at this, it will end up with something like the kind of social waste we show here and with a larger bureaucracy than is optimal.

Now consider the effect of the characteristics of bureaucracy pp. 21-23) on the equilibrium size of bureaucracy, as shown in Figure 1. The first thing to note is that the bureaucrats have a larger demand for the existence of bureaucracy than the average citizen, simply because it proivdes not only services for them but also jobs. Figure 2 shows the demand of the ordinary citizens and of the bureaucrats. The bureaucrats' demand is, of course, higher.

The government, which means the politicians, perceive the demand in practice as a combination of these two, depending on how many bureaucrats there are. The dotted line shows one such possible combination. A demand system which includes bureaucrats among the voters will thus demand more than would those voters who do not have jobs, depending on the provision of the service demand if left to themselves. Note that the strength of this effect depends on the number of bureaucrats. The politician will see the dotted line as closer to the demand of the bureaucrats if they make up a larger proportion of the population. Thus, we can have a dynamic process in which the increase in demand caused by bureaucrats leads to the hiring of more bureaucrats who increase the demand, which leads to the hiring of more bureaucrats, etc. It is not obvious that this process would end before 100 per cent of the population was employed as bureaucrats!

Note that the phenomenon shown in Figure 1, which would lead to the amount of bureaucratic services provided being in excess of the socially optimal amount, also applies to Figure 2. I have simply not drawn in the two additional triangles and the predicted outcome because the diagram is rather cluttered as it is. We would not, however, anticipate that the amount of the services provided would be the point where the dotted line crosses the cost line but somewhere well to the right of it.

Bureaucrats' power to inflate bureaucratic salaries

Bureaucrats would not only like to have big bureaucracy but also higher salaries. I am more familiar with the American statistics than

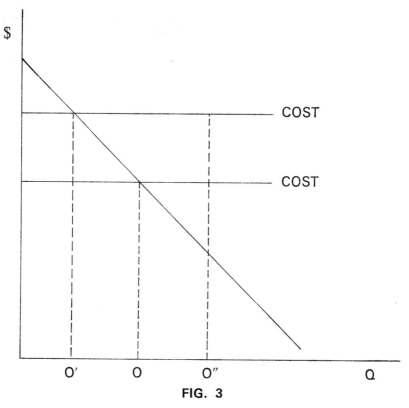

FIG. 3

with those of Britain but I suspect the situation is much the same in the two countries. In the United States federal civil servants are supposed to be paid wages comparable to those paid by private employers with similar labour. The comparison is made, however, by civil servants, and they are not biased against their own wages. Once again, we should not regard this attitude as particularly remarkable. They are human beings behaving in a very human way. But, regardless of our moral evaluation of the position, it would appear that they are paid about 30 per cent more than they would earn in private industry. In some cases these figures are really extra-ordinary. In New York City, for example, a garbage man is paid, counting everything, $16·47 per hour or about £9. In New York bad management seems to be endemic and I would not claim that equally absurd figures are found in all government jobs. It is, however, true that as a general rule there is a long line of people waiting for any vacancy in government employment, because the salary is so much ahead of the competing salary in private industry.

The effect is, of course, to raise costs. Figure 3, based on Figure 1, shows the demand and cost for a service, the demand curve being equivalent to the dotted line on Figure 2. The cost, granted you are overpaying your civil service by a considerable amount, is shown by the cost prime line. The optimum would be to pay the cost and purchase 0 units. Granted you are overpaying, however, the optimum number of units to be purchased would be 0'. Using the line of reasoning developed for Figure 1, however, we can see that the amount purchased would be 0", which is more than 0. It is more than 0 because I have drawn it that way. It is possible for the increased cost to be high enough so that, even with the expansion which comes from the phenomenon mentioned in connection with Figure 1, the total output is lower than it would be under optimal provision. This optimal provision includes the demand of bureaucrats for their jobs as well as the demand of the citizens. Although one could argue that the public service is being provided in smaller quantities than it should be, it is certainly being provided considerably in excess of what it should be, given its price. However, although the services are under-optimally supplied, the tax cost is certain to be higher.

The costs of bureaucracy

Bureaucrats are not pressed to work hard and be efficient. They can avoid pressure from above because they cannot be fired. This means not only that they are apt to be overpaid but also that they are inefficient in other senses: they do not seek the most efficient methods, they do not work hard, etc. Here again I am mostly familiar with the American data. It is a little hard to get cases in which governments directly compete with competing private industries because in general when the government undertakes an activity it makes it illegal for private enterprises to compete, or it funds its services entirely out of taxes and provides them 'free', with the result that a private competitor cannot hope to provide the service. There are some exceptions, however, and studies indicate considerable government inefficiency.[6] They show very considerably higher

---

[6] A number of these studies are collected in Robert M. Spann, 'Public Versus Private Provision of Governmental Service', in Thomas Borcherding (ed.). *Budgets and Bureaucrats: The Sources of Government Growth*, Duke University Press, Durham, NC, 1977.

costs when government provides a service than when it is provided privately. This is particularly surprising, since often the private industry which competes with the government is a regulated monopoly, well known to be relatively inefficient.

The net effect is much like the effect of the increase in wages and can also be shown on Figure 3. If we drew both of them in on the same figure the only difference would be that the cost' line would be still higher.

The exact cost inflicted on the citizenry because civil servants are (*a*) overpaid, and (*b*) relatively inefficient, is hard to compute. The rough rule of thumb is that it costs the government about twice as much as it would a private competitive producer. The only example I know of in which there is a clear-cut comparison of a government-provided service with a private, competitively-provided service concerns garbage collection in an area near Washington, DC.[7] It shows that private provision is about half as costly as government provision, although it is not obvious we should draw firm conclusions. The private fire departments which have sprung up in parts of the western United States also charge about half the cost of government fire departments for a similar service. I should not like to put too much emphasis on this figure. Still, it is amusing to consider what a GNP for most Western countries would be if the government sector were evaluated not at its resource cost but at one-half of it, which is what these figures would seem to indicate is about right.

IV. BUREAUCRATS' MONOPOLY OF INFORMATION

Bureaucrats naturally take advantage of their practical monopoly of information. One particularly striking example has to do with my previous remark about the labour cost of a New York garbage man. The salaries themselves are public information in the United States, but fringe benefits are frequently hard for the average citizen to evaluate. In the US we tend to think that fringe benefits will be somewhere around 30 per cent of wages, and the average citizen in New York probably thinks that is true of his governmental employees.

---

[7] James T. Bennett and Manley Johnson, 'Public Versus Private Provision of Collective Goods and Services: Garbage Collection Revisited', *Public Choice* (forthcoming).

For garbage men, the fringe benefits (included in the above hourly figure) are 78 per cent of their basic wage. For patrol men and firemen, the figure is even more extreme: slightly over 100 per cent in each case. This is an example of using the bureaucratic monopoly of information to get a much higher real wage than the apparent wage.

Another example, in some ways equally striking, concerns some rather technical provisions in the American Social Security legislation and regulations which make it possible for civil servants to add on to their regular and generous civil service pensions a Social Security pension at very little cost to themselves. These arrangements were for a long time unknown to anybody except civil servants. Now that they have become known it is very hard to explain them to the public. The civil servants not only have this quasi-monopoly of information, they are using every bit of their political power—very formidable in the United States—to retain this special privilege.

Once again we should not blame the bureaucrats for behaving in this ordinary human way, but we should take into account the effect of their behaviour. Their monopoly on information and their special facilities for lobbying are, of course, particularly important if there is some drive to improve bureaucratic efficiency. The bureaucrats are almost of necessity the only people who know the efficiency of a given bureau can be improved. They are extremely reluctant to do anything about it. Thus, the usual result of efforts to get further efficiency out of bureaucrats are statements that nothing can be done, together with suggestions that if the bureaucratic appropriation is only increased this year that will make it possible to make reductions in expenditures next year. When cuts are forced on the bureaucrats they are apt to allocate them in such a way as to maximise the pain felt by the voters rather than to improve efficiency. Only if it becomes obvious to them that they cannot get away with this tactic can we expect them to be efficient.

There was a very amusing example some years ago. Congress had reduced the budget of the customs service. The civil servant head of the appropriate part of the customs service laid off every customs inspector in the United States but not a single other employee of the bureau. He had, however, gone too far. Congress became annoyed, and he was transferred. Transferred, not fired! Certainly he was not sued for the damage and inconvenience he had caused by his quite extraordinary method of economising.

This was a by no means unique although extreme example. At the other end of the size spectrum, I was on the council of the American Political Science Association, which had been rather flush with funds and had used them to build up a sizeable bureaucracy in their Washington office. The days of wine and roses, however, were over, and it looked as if some cuts would be necessary. The permanent secretary suggested as the only way of making reductions that the small clerical office which handled subscriptions to journals be cut. None of the 'policy' officials were to be laid off, although it would be extremely difficult to specify what exactly they were doing. The cut, he suggested, would inconvenience the members and hence probably lead to its revocation.

Bureaucracy's gains and their costs to the community—one advantage

All of the factors listed above tend unfortunately to compound rather than to offset one another. The monopoly of information held by the bureaucrats, together with their special lobbying facility, makes it particularly easy for them to conceal either inefficiency or high wages. It also makes it easier for them to obtain the kind of gain shown in Figure 1. Further, their voting power makes it on the whole undesirable for politicians to attempt to cut through the smoke screen and get at the real structure. Last but not least, that in general they cannot be fired means that ultimately they can simply sabotage programmes to which they object. Altogether it is clear that they are in a position very substantially to expand the size of the bureaucracy.

There is one strong offsetting factor, which has appeared in a somewhat different format above: bureaucrats are under no strong incentive to be efficient, even when it comes to using the various techniques to expand or preserve the size of the bureaucracy. Indeed, on occasion they become tied up in routine and may turn down proposals which would permit a very considerable expansion, simply because it would entail a good deal of work to implement them. Thus, the laziness and inefficiency which is one of the characteristics of the bureaucrat[8] here has its advantage. It means that government services are not carried out as well as they otherwise would be, but it also means that the expansion of the bureaucracy

---

[8] Laziness is perhaps not the correct term. Some bureaucrats work very hard. In general, however, this hard work is not directly called for by their job and is either voluntary, a hobby on their part or the result of other members of the bureaucracy not pulling their weight.

is carried out less vigorously and efficiently than it would be with personnel who worked harder and more devotedly at their tasks.

I have been talking about *one* of the causes of the growth of government. The various bureaucratic factors discussed above are important in the growth of government, but I have no doubt there are many other causes of at least equal importance. If we want to stop the growth of government we should give very careful attention not only to the role of bureaucracy but also to the other causes.

V. HOW CAN WE CONTROL BUREAUCRACY?

What can be done to bring bureaucracy under better control?

1. An obvious first proposal is simply to reduce the scope of government and hence make the bureaucracy smaller. This is not easy. First, there is the bureaucracy's ability to defend itself and, secondly, there is, of course, a problem of differing philosophies of government.

2. There are a number of things one can do to reduce the size of bureaucracy without at the same time reducing the scope of governmental activity. An obvious one is simply to promote competition within the bureaucracy which denies the individual bureaucrat or the individual bureau the advantages in bargaining with the rest of the government (above). Suppose several regional bureaus handle public assistance payments. A parliament could note the cost of distributing the payments and the number of complaints they get from their constituents and decide that a particularly efficient bureau should get two more counties and a particular inefficient bureau get two less. After a few years one could anticipate the bureaus would pay much more attention to efficiency. We can go further. There is no reason why government activities cannot be contracted out provided only that we are careful to make sure they are contracted out to competing rather than to monopolistic companies.

3. High salary levels are harder to deal with. It may be that simply taking the bull by the horns and cutting wages until such time as voluntary resignations are about equal to applications from properly qualified people is the correct solution. I would anticipate that this policy would create quite a saving.

4. The voting power of bureaucrats is, of course, very difficult to handle in a democracy. In a country like Britain, which does not have a written constitution, it would at least be theoretically possible for parliament simply to provide that bureaucrats and their families did not vote, but I would think a better scheme would be to set up a set of special constituencies in which bureaucrats and their families elected—probably by proportional representation, so that different bureaus would get adequate representation—their own representatives to parliament, and did not vote in the geographical constituencies. This method would give them a weight in parliament roughly equivalent to their numbers but would also mean that they would face a very large number of MPs whose constituencies contained not a single bureaucrat.

All these suggestions are offered rather tentatively. I do not think the problem is insoluble, but it is certainly difficult.

Questions and Discussion

DR DUNCAN REEKIE (*University of Edinburgh*): I understand that the Civil Aviation Guilds in the USA have been pursuing a policy of de-regulation collectively in the last few years. Can you put this behaviour into your model, or are the bureaucrats of the CAG irrational?

PROF. TULLOCK: I originally thought this phenomenon was very difficult to explain. But, in the first place, it is a very small bureaucracy, and at the moment it is very easy to transfer one part of bureaucracy to another. Secondly, it is not the bureaucrats in the CAG but the political appointees at the top who appointed academics to implement the policy.

What is surprising to me is that there has not been more objection from the bureaucrats. A former graduate student of mine, James Miller, has been one of the principal people active in getting this policy through. He tells me that there simply is no cost to those bureaucrats transferred from one job to another in Washington, that is, the demand for bureaucrats is higher. But I am still somewhat surprised. So you are quite right. I regard that as an unfortunate test case.

LORD ROBBINS: In this country you could find many cases of that kind. At the outbreak of the Second World War a number of economists were recruited by the Office of the War Cabinet. They very speedily discovered that in all sorts of activities absolutely essential to the conduct of war, from the statistical point of view, conditions in Whitehall were lamentable.

with extreme reluctance to bring about the necessary enlargement of the various offices.

Furthermore, at the end of the war when, for reasons of policy, it was very clear that the Treasury, the senior department in the economic conduct of affairs, was palpably too small, the reluctance of the Treasury officials to consider any enlargement of its scope had to be seen to be believed.

PROF. TULLOCK: I am a little reluctant to talk about British conditions, but two things can happen. One is simply that, as I said earlier, people do not like their routines interrupted. But, secondly, I believe that in Britain the people who did not want this expansion were already at the top. You do not increase the number of field marshals very much if you go from three to five divisions, but you increase the number of major-generals a good deal. It is more trouble for the one existing field marshal. In this case, as a general rule, you are also not only suggesting that their power be *expanded* but also that their routines be very sharply *changed*. You are going to have them collecting statistics they are not accumstomed to. It might be necessary for them to get something a little better than the simple calculating machine they had learned how to use, and so on.

I have heard the same view from Professor Meade about his wartime office. Sir John Anderson was against expansion of his office. It is, however, true that at the end of the war the bureaucracy was very much larger than it had been at the beginning.

LORD ROBBINS: I would have thought almost necessarily so since we were, until 1935, more or less totally unprepared for war. Sir John Anderson was by common consent the most outstanding public servant of his day, and does not fit your picture very well.

PROF. TULLOCK: The National Science Foundation in the United States went on for many years without any increase in budget. This of course led to other people taking advantage of the opportunity, and all sorts of other government scientific funding projects cropped up all over the place. But I do not argue that everybody always fits the pattern or the theory. This view about the need for a large bureaucracy to fight a war is largely a myth. The United States moved from almost no army to two monster armies between 1860 and the beginning of 1861. The two armies were run with practically no headquarters. Most of their ammunition and other supplies were literally acquired from a procurer on the field of battle. The Baltimore and Ohio Railway, a major supplier for the Northern armies in the Eastern theatre, owned a bridge at Harper's Ferry which was destroyed 27 times during the course of the war. And there does not seem to have been anyone who thought that anybody except the Baltimore and Ohio Railway should be concerned: they were making a good return on shipping ammunition, which they did with great efficiency, charging a profitable price—they could put up their own bridge!

R. F. SANSOM (*Contractors' Plant Association*): May I reassure Professor Tullock that his view of bureaucracy is standardised in Britain. The conditions are very much the same as in the USA. I speak as a bureaucrat of some 20 years' standing in central and local government. By and large life in the public service is not subject to much harassment or pressure, except at the very top. The reluctance to expand at the very top may have as much to do with inter-departmental jealousies and inconvenience as any other factor.

To tame government I would have thought controlling money and men is the vital requirement. When I was in government service and indeed since then I have always been struck by the very low elasticity within it. It is very difficult to get people to transfer to other kinds of work even when there is a need. Somehow you end up with another cell in the hive and another drone. I do not know the reasons, but it is something to do with feeling that what you were doing in the past must have been necessary, and therefore it is faintly disreputable to be asked to stop it and do something else.

I suggest the only way in which you will tackle this tendency and reverse it is to get a grip on the total money resources and force politicians to choose between having more bureaucrats or spending more to get more votes. That would mean that if you want better salaries or more staff here you have got to save there. We must also attack this tradition of permanence. With increasing cries in Britain for comparability for public servants on everything, preferably only on the jobs that are paid better, this subject is ripe for stringent examination. So may I, first, confirm that most of this disease is here and, secondly, ask you where you think the point of attack can start? Is it Proposition 13? Is it, say, a 50 per cent marginal tax rate? Or what?

PROF. TULLOCK: There is a very old concept of budgeting, abandoned some time ago, in which instead of appropriating a given amount of cash for a given bureau, you assigned them a particular tax. And this compelled them to be efficient. They could usually keep the excess of tax over expenditure. If they turned out to be very efficient, the head of the bureau could take the tax and go to the Riviera. This led to more efficiency, although it also led to a rather elaborate lifestyle for the higher officials.

Now for the solutions and my own personal preference: I assume we are now talking about what is politically feasible. You know there are tax restrictions and such like being discussed in the United States. I am testifying before various committees in favour of them, but my own preference is different. It is to take various government agencies, of which we have a large number, let us say the Post Office, for example, and give it free to its employees on the understanding that they own it but do not have any right to further subsidy. My hypothesis is that this solution would get rid of about two-thirds of modern government without too much political kick-back because the employees, at least at first, would feel benefited rather than injured, and the taxpayer would get rid of what is now quite a significant subsidy as one of his expenses. In practice I suspect the employees would then do a reasonably good job of running it. But we are now talking about practical politics and I do not claim very high expertise in that field.

CECIL MARGOLIS (*North Yorkshire County Council*): The main difficulty is that there is a kind of conspiracy between the thousands of officials who are more or less permanent and the elected members. For example, I recently attended a seminar in North Yorkshire at which the Education Officer tried to justify the continuation of the establishment of schools, and even building new schools, when there is an expected fall in the school population. I pointed out this contrast between the demand for school places and the supply and was reprimanded by the Chairman of the Policy and Resources Committee, one of the elected people on the Council. How do I deal with this problem?

PROF. TULLOCK: Unfortunately this is something you cannot avoid in democratic government. There is a way out if you have committees in your county. In France, members of committees, i.e. local politicians, instead of being permitted to choose their own committees, which means that the members are all from the special interest groups, are assigned to committees by a system of random selection, and have to change every two years. This, however, is a minor reform—it would make things work better, but not very much. Basically you are simply pointing to an unfortunate characteristic of democracy, but I do not think there is anything we can do about it.

PROF. D. R. MYDDELTON: One suggestion Mr Sansom made is completely wrong: the idea that you could reduce government bureaucracy by cutting the top rate of income tax to 50 per cent. The whole point about these high rates of personal income tax is that they do not raise much or any revenue. When we discuss cutting bureaucracy we are talking about substantial cuts in government spending and therefore substantial cuts in government revenue. Cutting the top rate of tax would probably actually *increase* revenue—it certainly would not cost anything.

PROF. IVOR PEARCE (*University of Southampton*): I was wondering, in connection with restricting the money available to governments, if they are right to sell bonds, in an indiscriminate way, to raise money which can then be squandered. Should we introduce the rule, which used to be talked about, namely that, if we do not want to run an unbalanced deficit budget, then government must raise money by selling bonds only for the purpose of investment in income-earning industries, so that it has a real asset that will earn income, which will pay the interest on the bonds. To allow them to do anything else is to allow them to squander the wealth of future generations.

LORD ROBBINS: Decisions of that sort are ministerial, not bureaucratic. We have just had a tremendous scandal revealed through one of the newspapers—it was the *Guardian*, I think—which reported a letter from the head of the Treasury protesting against various expenditures, sanctioned by Ministers.[1] I think that, regarding the pickle we are in on the financial side, so far as decision-making is concerned the blame rests 100 per cent on Ministers of both parties.

PROF. TULLOCK: Of course, the bureaucrats by their votes can have some effect on who is the Minister.

LORD ROBBINS: In Britain we make a clear distinction between the various grades. There is no doubt at all that the lower-paid public servants are very highly organised, and at the moment are in an extremely intransigent mood. It is not true, judging by the history of our public service, that up to recently their pay was equivalent to what most of them could have earned in private enterprise. The present position in which they have index-linked pensions and have done rather well is of recent origin. It was not initiated by them, but by a committee presided over by a man universally respected for his impartiality and his intellect, Lord Boyle. This is just an accident.

PROF. TULLOCK: But who provided the papers for the committee?

LORD ROBBINS: In the past our top civil servants were underpaid compared with private enterprise.

PROF. TULLOCK: It is not clear to me whether the top men were underpaid relatively to what they could earn elsewhere. But if you take, let us say, a Class 1 civil servant in the Department of Defense, he may be handling a segment which, if he were in private industry, would give him a salary of $250-300,000 a year—he is not making anywhere near that much. It is not obvious that he would necessarily be capable of making

---

[1] ['£800m losses predicted for "job" projects', *Guardian*, 28 February 1979: reported 'leak' of a letter from Sir Douglas Wass, Permanent Secretary to the Treasury, to Sir Peter Carey, Permanent Secretary to the Department of Industry.—ED.]

$250,000 in private industry. A man who starts in a specialised part of a bureaucracy and rises to the top may have the whole of his experience in that service; he may not be able to switch over quickly and start manufacturing automobiles. In any event, I would be in favour of raising the salaries of the top $\frac{1}{2}$ per cent of the bureaucracy, preferably firing the present top $\frac{1}{2}$ per cent and hiring a fresh top $\frac{1}{2}$ per cent. But they are really a sort of froth on the whole. Have postal clerks, for example, always been underpaid in Britain? If so, why were they taking the job? In the United States we have an immense queue of five or six years between examinations for the Post Office because it takes five or six years to work off the number who pass. And I should say the last time, in an outburst of inanity, they were compelled to fill out their examination papers 16 times, and none of them objected to this idiocy.

OLIVER STUTCHBURY: Could I ask Professor Tullock about the operation of what I think are called 'sunset acts'?

PROF. TULLOCK: I regard them as largely a fake. The specific proposal, which has been enacted by some state legislatures, is that, say, every five years, you have a rotating schedule in which the legislature must consider whether a given bureau should be abolished. In practice it is put rather in the other form: it must be considered whether the bureau should be re-created in essence. But, in the first place, that is the way our budget works anyway—every year the whole budget has to be passed. It is an invention which *sounds* good and little more. Compelling people to think about the matter in a formal way every five years may be helpful, but my guess is it will turn out to be purely and simply a formality.

J. S. FAIRBAIRN (*M. & G. Securities*): In times of what is regarded as high unemployment, job creation has a good patriotic ring about it. Is it not possible that many bureaucrats see it as being good for the commonwealth by creating jobs, by if you like recruiting more.

PROF. TULLOCK: There are special circumstances, for example, at the bottom of the slump in 1933, when this would literally have been true. They might not be optimising the use of labour but simply creating a job for which they were going to pay by printing money. In January 1933 in the United States—I think you were beyond the bottom by then, but we were right at the bottom—it would have been a positive social act. It might not have been the best way of spending the money, but I think they sometimes do feel this way. Still, I think almost uniformly they are mistaken.

3. Macro-economic Controls on Government

A. P. L. MINFORD
University of Liverpool

The Author

A. P. L. Minford: Edward Gonner Professor of Applied Economics, University of Liverpool, since 1976. Formerly Visiting Hallsworth Research Fellow, University of Manchester, 1974-75. Sometime Consultant to the Ministry of Overseas Development, Ministry of Finance (Malawi), Courtaulds, Treasury, British Embassy (Washington). Editor of *National Institute Economic Review*, 1975-76. Author of *Substitution Effects, Speculation and Exchange Rate Stability* (1978), and of essays published in *Inflation in Open Economies* (1976); *The Effects of Exchange Adjustments* (1977); *On How to Cope with Britain's Trade Position* (1977); *Contemporary Economic Analysis* (1978).

Preliminary remarks

I would like to start by expressing my delight that Lord Robbins is here today as our chairman.

I was recently reading an account of his inter-war disagreements with Lord Keynes, especially over Keynes's rising protectionism, and, while I realise he may retract some of his views of that time, I nevertheless found that they had a very relevant and prescient ring to them. They constantly re-assert underlying long-run realities as against the opportunism of the short-run palliative. As the chickens of two decades of such palliatives come home to roost, we are learning, I hope, to pay principal attention to these realities.

I. INTRODUCTION

For the bulk of the last two decades, the economic affairs of Britain have been seriously mismanaged. Dissatisfaction with that mis-management has now, as we approach the 1980s, reached a peak. We survey an economy with rampant inflation, poor productivity and low wages. Perhaps we are at a watershed where institutions and practices will be radically changed. Other speakers have given an analysis of government behaviour and where it has gone wrong, and have talked about alternative legal frameworks and constitutional reform.

I shall concentrate on the economic content this framework should embody. Indeed, if a government came along that would implement this *content,* I am naïve enough to believe it would be so welcomed by the people that our *practices* would have reformed themselves without a far-reaching overhaul of the legal framework.

II. PROPOSALS: SUMMARY

Restrictions have to be imposed on the government's fiscal and monetary actions, whether through self-discipline encouraged by new conventions or by legal means. They concern (i) the budget, (ii) the money supply, and (iii) the structure of taxation and social security.

(i) *The budget* should be balanced on a 'normal year basis'. This means not that each year should be balanced, but that it should be balanced when allowance is made for the cyclical position of the economy and for any agreed stabilisation element in fiscal policy (discussed later). This would imply that the average budget would be in balance over several years taken together.

(ii) *The money supply* should grow at a rate sufficient to finance the normal growth of output, again on a normal year basis. In this case, the adjustment should be only for any agreed stabilisation rule.

(iii) *The structure of taxes and benefits* should be set according to three broad principles:
- (a) some minimum income must be assured (the safety net) to any household, but for those with able-bodied members it should be significantly *below* the income from unskilled work;
- (b) the marginal tax rate above this minimum income should not rise above 50 per cent at *any* point;
- (c) the base of taxation should be expenditure, not income.

This structure should not be altered for stabilisation reasons. Any fiscal stabilisation should occur through neutral variations in an expenditure tax. The nearest approximation at present is VAT. There should not be, for example, variations in personal or corporate marginal tax rates or commodity tax rates which exert disproportionate pressure on particular sectors or groups.

(iv) *Stabilisation policy*, within this framework, should be *automatic* not discretionary, and the rules by which it is governed should be *published*. There seems to be a defensible case for the following types of stabilisers:
- (a) Tax rates should be fixed, not tax revenue as at present. Hence there would be an automatic tendency for the budget deficit to fall as activity rises and *vice-versa*;
- (b) If output is expected to rise above its 'natural' level, VAT or the general expenditure tax rate should be raised and *vice-versa* —the standard 'regulator';
- (c) If prices are expected to accelerate, the growth of the money supply should be reduced, and *vice-versa*.

Finally, the best sort of stabiliser is competitive markets for goods and labour where prices and wages are flexible. Compared with this optimum stabiliser, the use of fiscal and monetary policy to reduce the swings in output and prices is very much a second best. The institutional rigidities imposed by the present government/union/ corporation structure are unlikely to be removed sufficiently rapidly for us to be able to rely solely on the competitive mechanism for some time to come. Nevertheless, the ultimate aim of stabilisation policy should be its own withering away through progress towards flexible and competitive markets.

III. THE FOUR RESTRICTIONS/REFORMS

(i) BUDGETARY POLICY

So used have we become to the language and habits of intervention that the reforms I have described are likely to appear extreme as well as impracticable. Yet we have already travelled some way along this road, as we can recognise by asking whether, ten years ago, it would have been conceivable that there should be targets for the Public Sector Borrowing Requirement (PSBR) and the money supply, least of all when unemployment was over 5 per cent of the labour force. Of course it would not have been. These policies have emerged partly as a necessary minimum response to the accelerating inflation of the last decade, and partly as a result of an intellectual counter-attack on the post-war Keynesian consensus.[1] Those in government who blame the financial markets for this slight discipline are deluding us; they know in their hearts that, if the financial markets did not exist, they would have had to invent some other excuse for following these policies. Some of them may still believe that incomes policy provides an alternative, but they must be a dwindling band in the face of exhaustive empirical (and causal) evidence that incomes policy lowers neither inflation nor unemployment; I refer to the findings presented in the volume edited by Professors Michael Parkin and Michael Sumner,[2] to a recent article by Brian Henry and Paul Ormerod,[3] and to some work of mine

---

[1] IEA Papers have played a leading part in this re-educational process, starting with *Not Unanimous* in 1959 and including a classic statement by Milton Friedman in *Counter-Revolution in Monetary Theory*, Occasional Paper 33, 1970.

[2] (eds.) *Incomes Policy and Inflation*, Manchester University Press, 1972.

[3] 'Incomes Policy and Wage Inflation: Empirical Evidence for the UK, 1961-77', *NIESR Review*, August 1978.

reported recently at the Association of University Teachers of Economics (AUTE) conference.[4]

(ii) THE MONETARIST APPROACH

The framework I have described belongs to the school of thought known loosely as monetarism. This embraces a variety of approaches to the economy, all of which, however, share the propositions that there is a stable long-run demand for money, that there is a long-run connection between the supply of money and the budget deficit, and that output tends towards a long-run equilibrium set by the availability of resources. It is important to emphasise this common core of thought in the monetarist position, because, whatever differences may occur on details of policy prescription, it engenders a basic agreement on the broad direction and objectives of policy.

Role of expectations

Nevertheless, the propositions I have set out emerge, in the precise form given, from a monetarist model in which the important assumption is made that people and firms use the information available to them in a sensible manner to forecast the likely shape of the economic environment. This assumption, of 'rational' expectations, has been notably pioneered in the context of macro-economic models by Professors Robert Lucas and Thomas Sargent in the US.[5] Unfortunately, economists in this country (as opposed to the US where it is taken very seriously indeed) have been slow to accept this assumption. They have preferred the earlier conventional wisdom that people form their expectations by some automatic rule of thumb relating future values to past values (so-called 'adaptive' expectations); hence that they can be systematically misled by policy-makers and can systematically make the same type of forecast errors, year in year out.

---

[4] A. P. L. Minford, and M. Brech, 'The Wage Equation and Rational Expectations', AUTE Conference, March 1979, Working Paper No. 7901. Dept. of Economics, University of Liverpool.

[5] E.g. R. E. Lucas, Jnr., 'Econometric testing of the Natural Rate Hypothesis', in O. Eckstein (ed.), *The Econometrics of Price Determination*, Federal Reserve Board of Governors, Washington DC, 1970; and T. J. Sargent, 'Rational Expectations, the Real Rate of Interest and the Natural Rate of Unemployment', *Brookings Papers on Economic Activity*, Brookings Institution, Washington DC, 1973.

'Cottoning-on' through rational expectations

This proposition is palpably absurd as well as—dare I say it—abominably patronising. The expression 'rational expectations' is perhaps ill-chosen for the assumption I have described, carrying overtones of supermen plugged into computerised models of the economy. Yet these overtones are exaggerated. The essence of the idea is quite simply that people and firms 'cotton on' to publicly-known changes in the economic environment, especially in economic policy.

This 'cottoning on' is important because the basic mechanism by which budgets have been thought to stimulate the economy is one in which output rises, and inflation occurs *later*, once the economy is overheated. Yet if people *anticipate* the overheating, the inflation occurs *at once*, and the output rise does not occur because the stimulus dissipates itself in inflation. In fact, these immediate inflationary effects may cause output to fall through the associated financial crisis, marked by sharply rising interest rates, falling share prices, liquidity shortages and so on.

Balanced budget plus money supply target

Seen in this way, the key requirement for eliminating inflation is the confidence that the budget will be balanced on the average. The money supply target that goes with budget balance is one where money supply matches growth in output. These long-run or average targets reflect the equilibrium of the economy. Experience shows that in equilibrium with low inflation, the private sector is not prepared to absorb net financial assets[6] (i.e. public sector debt of any sort) in significant amounts (credit for initially focussing on this important point must go to Mr Wynne Godley)[7]. The counterpart

---

[6] Another way of putting this is to say that the private sector has a demand for public debt in its portfolio of assets, but that in 'normal' non-inflationary circumstances it would not wish to increase its holdings of this debt faster than its holdings of other assets, especially physical assets. Thus the vast proportion of its savings will be devoted to investment in goods, and only a small proportion is available for investment in public debt. Evidence bearing on this is given in my paper, 'A rational expectations model of the UK under fixed and floating exchange rates', forthcoming in Proceedings of April 1979 Carnegie-Rochester conference on 'The State of Macro-economics', eds. K. Brunner and A. H. Meltzer.

[7] E.g., F. Cripps and W. Godley, 'Formal Analysis of the Cambridge Economic Policy Group Model', *Economica*, 1976.

of this discovery is that government cannot issue these assets (including and particularly, the monetary component) through a deficit.

Mechanism of inflation

Inflation occurs when the government through a deficit issues assets in *excess* of what the private sector will absorb. The private sector will only absorb these financial assets in so far as inflation cuts the real value of its existing assets and so forces it to acquire new assets in order to maintain its real stock of them. In principle this inflation occurs *via* a spending mechanism. The private sector gets rid of financial assets it does not desire by spending them on goods, domestic and foreign, until prices are driven up sufficiently to produce the necessary inflation at which they will absorb the assets created by the deficit. However, in practice this mechanism is 'short-circuited' by expectations; since there is a general expectation that inflation *will* occur, there is an *immediate* impact on all those areas of contracting which must take notice of future inflation, i.e. across all financial markets, labour markets and goods markets. Interest rates rise, the exchange rate drops, wage increases accelerate, and prices are marked up more rapidly—at once. We recognise these symptoms in the financial crisis brought about by a rise in the PSBR. Such 'confidence' crises mark both an acceleration in prices and a faltering of the real economy.

After the crisis, if the government persists with its deficit, the economy gradually settles down at a higher rate of inflation and interest rates, the real economy returns to normal, with contracts in effect being indexed at the higher inflation rate. There is nevertheless an important waste of resources in this inflationary world, both because a monetary economy works most efficiently when money has a constant value and because the inflation rate is in practice not fixed but variable and uncertain. Geoffrey Hilliard and I have tried to measure these costs in a recently published paper.[8] We found them to be apparently of considerable significance.

The UK is at present in such a situation. It is essential that the processes I have described be put into reverse. The long-run targets of a zero PSBR and output—matching growth in money supply are the essential ingredients of an inflation-free economy.

---

[8] 'The Costs of Variable Inflation', in M. J. Artis and A. R. Nobay, *Contemporary Economic Analysis*, Croom Helm, 1978.

The transition from stagnation to stabilisation

But this is a gathering of practical men. 'Yes', you may perhaps agree, 'in the long run this is so. But how do we get there from our present stagnation? Will not cuts in the deficit and the money supply aggravate unemployment without reducing inflation significantly in the short?' I have discussed these worries above, theoretically. Perhaps it will be more impressive to reflect on the experience following the December 1976 IMF measures. Many feared these would be savagely deflationary. In the event they had a rapid effect on the rate of inflation, while output continued to grow in 1977 at about 2 per cent per annum. In 1978 growth picked up to over 3 per cent.

Yet these effects would have been more 'virtuous' still if the government had not made two mistakes of execution. First, they resisted the appreciation of sterling in 1977 and so slowed down the emergence of lower inflation. Secondly, they caused massive underspending in the financial year 1977-78, causing the PSBR to be some £3 billion lower in outcome than intended. Such *unanticipated* shortfalls *are* as deflationary as traditionally feared, because they have no impact on inflationary expectations until long after they have occurred. Hence a PSBR cut brought about by underspending gives the worst of both worlds: a cut in output but not in inflation.

On the question of the transition from stagnation to stabilisation, the answer is that you should try to get the best of both worlds: announce the phased programme of eliminating the PSBR over, say, three to four years, start implementing it immediately to give it full credibility, and reap the benefits of sharply reduced inflation expectations while minimising the traditionally deflationary consequences of expenditure cuts along the transition path. It is quite likely that the virtuous effects on output of the better monetary and financial environment will outweigh these deflationary effects. At the worst, there will be insignificant effects on output with rapid benefits in lower inflation.

The rate of exchange

A word in passing on the exchange rate. Too much attention is paid to initial symptoms in the transmission mechanism by which inflation is reduced on the back of a stronger exchange rate in an improved financial environment.[9] It is true, there is a temporary period in

---

[9] The London Business School team led by Dr Terry Burns has done much useful work on this mechanism: see its monthly *Economic Outlooks*.

which margins are squeezed in the traded goods sector. But both economic theory and the empirical evidence suggests strongly that trade flows respond to exchange rates when changes in margins or competitiveness are thought to be long-lasting.

International trade cannot turn on a dime, there are significant adjustment costs in building up an export line or switching sources of supply. Hence a strong exchange rate brought about temporarily as inflation is reduced will not affect trade flows significantly, precisely because they are temporary; the exchange rate strengthens until interest rates move into line and after this competitiveness returns to its normal condition at the new lower rate of inflation.

(iii) TAXATION

I have talked so far about average long-run targets for the budget and money supply and about the problems of transition. But it is as important to get the structure of taxation right for the real economy as are these monetary aspects for the efficient monetary working of the economy. On these matters, I would cite the growing consensus among public finance economists on the potential effects on incentives of our high marginal tax rates at both the lower and upper ends of our tax and benefit system. The general conclusion is that the income redistribution effects of these high marginal rates are either negligible or best achieved, if desired, in other ways, while the disincentive effects are potentially serious enough to warrant removal —even if the empirical evidence on exactly how strong they are is difficult to disentangle.

A further distortion of the savings/investment decision can be avoided by moving the base of taxation from an income to an expenditure basis, with little administrative difficulty.[10]

(iv) STABILISATION RULES

I turn now to the matter of stabilisation policy.

Some monetarists have argued that government should not attempt to stabilise the economy by varying the budget deficit or the money supply in response to their perception of economic trends. I have argued this myself in the past. Various reasons have been advanced. Professor Milton Friedman argued that, given an in-

---

[10] As argued by the 'Meade Report', Institute of Fiscal Studies, *The Structure and Reform of Direct Taxation,* Allen & Unwin, 1978.

adequate knowledge of the relationships in the economy, such 'stabilisation policy' was more likely to worsen variations around trend in output and inflation. More recently, Professor Sargent has argued—from a rational expectations viewpoint—that such policies will have no effect on output variation and may *worsen* inflation variation. He has also argued[11] that from a welfare point of view, even if they could reduce output variation, these policies would reduce welfare generally by interfering with individuals' planned decisions.

These are a diverse bunch of arguments, and they are not all consistent with one another.

My own still tentative experience in working with a rational expectations model of the UK economy is that simple stabilisation rules, if known by everybody and practised consistently by government, *can* reduce the variation in output and inflation in response to shocks. This arises because Professor Sargent's model appears not to fit the evidence as well as some alternative theories of wage and price formation. Turning to Milton Friedman's argument I would say these rules would be better than nothing provided the government's forecasts are no worse than other people's, which seems a reasonable assumption.

More competition required

On the question of welfare, the crucial assumption is that the economy would in the absence of these rules be in an optimal position. This assumption is hard to sustain, though it would be true if goods and labour markets were competitive. We must fight hard for more competitiveness in markets which must in practice be the best stabilisation mechanism of all, as I argued earlier. Many vested interests, and not only trade unions, oppose this solution, and they must be resisted. Nevertheless, if and until it is achieved, fiscal and monetary stabilisation policy can probably make a modest contribution.

In what way? First, few would argue with the proposition that tax *rates* should be fixed, to give an automatic stabiliser response to the budget deficit. If tax revenues were fixed, output shocks would be

---

[11] In chapter 16 of *Macro-economic Theory,* Academic Press, New York (forthcoming). For a similar argument, see also Michael Beenstock, *The Foreign Exchanges: Theory, Modelling and Policy,* Macmillan, 1978.

substantially magnified, because as output fell tax rates would *rise* imparting further downward pressure to output.

Secondly, a simple tax regulator turns out to be capable of dampening fluctuations in output if it is varied in response to expected output. This dampening comes about because real wages in particular are slow to adjust themselves to a change in the equilibrium real wage, and adjust very little to temporary changes in output. Hence it is employment rather than relative prices that takes the burden of adjustment to changes in demand. And this means that the stabilisation of those changes in demand will help to stabilise output.

Thirdly, the money supply should vary *inversely* with the expected rate of inflation to dampen the effect of shocks on the inflation rate which may be exaggerated by the reaction of financial conditions. As inflation rises, the demand for money drops with higher interest rates, hence, if money supply growth is not *cut,* it has to be absorbed by a *further* rise in inflation. It is best therefore to *cut* the money supply growth rate when inflation is expected to rise, and *vice-versa.* This is the opposite of an 'accommodative' monetary policy, which is dangerous in that it severely aggravates swings in inflation. Notice however that much of the usual policy discussion assumes that you should *raise* the money supply in response to higher inflation. This notion is quite wrong.

The importance of these rules should not be exaggerated. They are somewhat helpful, but are not necessary in any way to ensure that the economy reaches equilibrium. It will do that by itself. I must also emphasise that these must be *rules* for government response, they cannot be varied quixotically from year to year or month to month according to the government's whim, in the manner of so-called 'fine tuning'. Any deviation from the rule will unambiguously worsen the economy's performance, because it will add to the unpredictable elements that disturb private plans.

New truths?—the lessons of experience

It is sometimes said to me, 'All well and fine, but why weren't you and others saying all this 10 or 20 years ago?' The first part of the answer is that in the micro-economic workings of markets, many of us have been convinced for a long time by the evidence from a multitude of empirical studies that market prices do have their supposed effect on demands and supplies. Within the economics profession, as pointed out by Professor Littlechild, the growing *consensus* (fostered by the IEA) for at least a decade, perhaps longer, has been that markets work.[12] This consensus has been resisted primarily by *non*-economists—especially by politicians who learned their economics in the inter-war or largely post-war period (from the wrong people and not from Lord Robbins!), and, I should add, by business men.

The second part of the answer concerns demand management and macro-economics. Here there has been a change in perceptions dating from the mid-1960s, in the US and the mid-1970s in the UK. (In Europe there has been less change either way.) Why? Because, I think, crude 'Keynesian' policies were not pushed to their ultimate logic in the US until the 'New Deal' policies of the Kennedy-Johnson administration and Vietnam, and in the UK until we floated the exchange rate in 1972 and threw off the constraints of world-inflation on our inflation rate. These (*un*controlled) experiments brought home the flaws in the Keynesian model more clearly than any amount of academic work. In the UK many of us, notably of course Professors Alan Walters, David Laidler and Michael Parkin, were convinced well before 1972 that 'money mattered', but some (I among them) did not foresee then how it would work, with a floating exchange rate, to drive inflation up so rapidly and to have little effect on output, even in the short run.

The rational expectations view I have set out today is the theoretical response of economists to the rapidity with which inflation has followed on the heels of Keynesian expansion policies once the fetters of long-run budget targets or fixed exchange rates were taken off them. The irony is that, if Keynesian policies are operated *within* the fetters of long-run targets, they can help moderately to stabilise the economy, as I have argued.

IV. CONTROL OF GOVERNMENT EXPENDITURE

I end with some remarks about methods of organising public spending. We have had much discussion in recent years of cash limits and methods of planning public spending. There is no magic in any *method* of implementing principles. The principles are most important,

---

[12] Documented by Samuel Brittan in a survey of economists, *Is There an Economic Consensus?: An Attitude Survey,* Macmillan, 1973.

and then the method must be *efficient*. The principles are that policies should be orientated towards the targets for the PSBR and the money supply as discussed. On that basis, efficient methods would have various ingredients including: proper cash flow planning and monitoring, forward projections of departmental spending to ensure smooth execution of programmes (interruptions raise costs), and as good forecasts as possible of the PSBR, the economy and so forth. Cash limits have a role in efficient cash planning, as do the estimates with which they are appropriately to be integrated. So does a properly set out Government White Paper on Expenditure and Revenues. So do forecasts from all quarters including the government. And so on. But we should not make the mistake of thinking that cash limits, announced from on high, so to speak, can *on their own* do anything. If they flow from policy realities, they will reinforce those realities, as would any well-executed method, but they are not a substitute for political will, the reality itself.

I have left open the question of how these constraints on government behaviour in macro-policy would be achieved. It remains my hope that the next democratically-elected government will accept them as natural and appropriate, that they will set us on a new course, and that their successors will follow it. If they do, we can save ourselves and the constitutional lawyers a lot of trouble. I leave you with that hope.

Questions and Discussion

C. M. JACKSON (*Spillers*): You commented on the effect on the small economy of having fixed exchange rates. Could there be any benefit for this country from accepting a fixed exchange rate with the European Currency Union (ECU), for example, in the context of the European Community?

PROF. MINFORD: That very much depends on the manner of the fixing, the manner of the transitional arrangements, and so on. If the only liberty that a floating exchange rate gives you is the liberty to choose your own inflation rate, then it is best exercised either by choosing a zero inflation rate and floating against inflation in the other countries, or, if other countries are prepared to settle on a zero inflation rate in some pre-agreed way or some natural way due to pressures of some sort, then by joining as wide as possible a currency area, because of the reduction of transaction costs in the use of money, etc., that this involves. So I think the answer to the ECU question has to be that, if it can be centred on a strong currency/low inflation economy, there is no objection at all to our converging on its inflation rate and tending towards a stable exchange rate with it.

The transition arrangements have, of course, to be very carefully handled. The problems that arise with fixed but adjustable exchange rates are in terms of appalling instability as you reach the margins of intervention, which can in practice destabilise policy itself. Some people, for example, have suggested that we should devalue massively in order to enter the European Monetary System (EMS) and then hold the new exchange rate stable. There could be no worse prescription for disaster than that, because it would destabilise the monetary targets, the anti-inflationary policy, and so on. So the answer to your very good question is: Yes, with the right transitional arrangements and provided we are all converging on the right low inflation rate.

CHRISTOPHER JOHNSON (*Lloyds Bank*): I wonder whether Professor Minford is not in effect advocating that government should become more ferocious rather than more tame? His recipes, while admirable in principle, require a degree of toughness by either the Treasury or the Bank of England, because whoever is going to carry out this policy would have to be very much tougher than previous governments, and possibly fly against what people really want. All of us may want inflation to be cured, but are people as a whole prepared to pay the price?

Professor Minford is adopting a rather extreme version of the crowding-out argument. He is assuming there is a large fund of savings which the government is now borrowing and which would otherwise be taken up by the private sector. We would all like to think it was so. There is some demand for investment funds from industry, but how fast would it increase in the circumstances he describes? It seems to me that his PSBR rule would increase the supply of savings for the private sector. His expenditure tax would go in the same direction; if effective it would probably encourage savings and discourage consumption. The effect of these two policies would be to generate an enormous balance-of-payments surplus, possibly with large overseas investment helped by exchange control. I am not sure how much it would raise output in our own economy.

On the control of the money supply: I think recent research has shown that the demand for money in Britain is unstable. The Bank of England found what looked like a good equation for M1, but I suspect it has begun to break down massively in the last two years. The OECD found a reasonable equation for M3 in every major country except the UK—they simply could not find one in the last eight years. But we do in practice have something like a stabilising device for the money supply, even though the demand for money is fairly unpredictable. When it threatens to get out of hand the effect in the short run is that, for those next few months, the money supply target is reduced in order to get it back on to an annual figure of 12 per cent. If you have 16 per cent for one quarter, you have got to come down perhaps to below 8 per cent for the next quarter.

MINFORD: I was not taken entirely by surprise by Mr Johnson's question. On the short-run price to be paid I have argued that it comes very much out of the type of expectations mechanism you use. The traditional idea that a cut in the budget deficit must cut output immediately, and then gradually over time the labour markets and goods markets and so forth will show less overheating, and this will gradually show up in lower inflation, is something that, although we have all got very used to it, arises only in a particular type of model, namely one where people learn very slowly about the way in which the system is changing. But this is precisely where I wish to take issue with this model. I think that our experience shows that people learn much more rapidly about changes in policy in the financial and inflationary environment. Most notably, of course, we have seen it in the behaviour of the exchange rate, where the London Business School has done a lot of very interesting analysis which has shown that it reacts very rapidly to the money supply. We have also seen it in financial markets. If the PSBR changes, we see that interest rates move very rapidly to discount its future level. So I would argue that this question depends very much on how you set up your theory of expectations and how you expect them to be influenced.

Essentially the same issue is that of crowding out. If you accept that there are rapid effects in financial markets on interest rates and exchange rates and so forth, you also find that there is an effect when you analyse the empirical evidence of these financial changes on the main categories of expenditure, consumption and investment, but particularly consumption. A lot of work is now converging—there is some even in the Treasury —to the effect that inflation has a significant negative effect on consumption. I would think it also clearly has an effect on stock-building and certain elements of investment that are very sensitive to financial conditions, liquidity, and so forth. When you add all these effects together I would say you have in effect a situation where if you raise the PSBR you create a financial crisis—you depress private expenditure to a very considerable extent.

I do not want to get hooked on the question of whether that effect is either more or less than the original, traditional, stimulus. This is an empirical matter—there is some evidence one way and some evidence the other; but we know that these temporary short-run effects are not nearly as severe, they are very uncertain and probably not very strong compared with the effects on inflation of a change in policy. So I do not think there is a massive price to be paid by pursuing better policies, and I do not think that there is a severe short-run problem. I do not think we should therefore see it in those terms.

On the demand for money and whether it is stable, I should have emphasised that the question is really one of the long-run stability of the demand for money rather than whether it shifts about a little bit in the short run. I grant there is quite a lot of evidence that money demand functions have been rather volatile in both the US and the UK, and in other countries, and this is clearly a problem if you are trying to stabilise the supply of money on a day-to-day basis. I would not argue for that; I never have. I would argue that what you need to do is to stabilise the expected growth of the money supply, and this involves a very different sort of framework. It involves setting a framework of long-run stability within which you can tolerate deviations. So I think we can get around that problem.

DR BARRY BRACEWELL-MILNES (*Erasmus University, Rotterdam*): One major fault of the contra-cyclical management of the economy in the period since the war has been that, for reasons of timing delays, the effect has more often been perverse than desired. It has been more pro-cyclical in its consequences than contra-cyclical. Where Professor Minford speaks of stabilising the economy, and not in the sense of a consistent long-term policy but up-and-down variations from time to time, it seems to me that his proposals are open to precisely the same objection.

MINFORD: The difference between the sort of stabilising feedback rules I am talking about and traditional demand management policy is that these forecasts will be public information throughout the system. And the feedback rules themselves will be public. In the previous policies nobody knew what the government might do. They might be able to deduce some rule but there was so much variance surrounding it, so many deviations on a year-by-year basis, that it was a very unpredictable business. Secondly, of course, the forecasts were kept secret and there was not much competition in the very early days in the form of forecasts. So the framework really is one where publicly-available forecasts lead to a publicly-known response by government. And the sorts of simulations I have done with models which incorporate that sort of publicly-known rule suggest that it would be stabilising. In other words, everyone would have the same forecast and everyone would know that the government would be reacting in a certain way to it. It would be very different from the previous discretionary rules.

SAMUEL BRITTAN (*Financial Times*): I have one specific question and one general observation leading to another question. The specific question is: What does Professor Minford think of the effects of what some people call cosmetic cuts in the PSBR? The archetypal example is the selling of BP shares so that there is a change in the source of financing, and it looks good. But this is not a hypothetical—I will not say, in this audience, an academic—question. Mr Healey has just told us that if he had been able to present a budget he would have looked for cuts in spending which 'don't affect employment'. And I would have thought it would have been some kind of financial cosmetic device of this kind. We also know that a Conservative Government would, in the so-called interval before it can cut public spending, also look for these devices. Incidentally, the Budget that Mr Healey did not present and the Budget the Conservatives are muttering about seem to me to be almost identical and to employ many of the same gimmicks. Possibly the reason is that they are talking to some of the same financial people. But I would very much like Professor Minford's view on what the effects of such cosmetic cuts are, both in the long and the short run, in the present policy framework and under his suggested alternative.

Secondly, I am sympathetic to but worried about the idea of rules for government response which are published, as it were, on tablets, and which we all know about and do not change according to the government's whim. Philosophically I am very much in favour of rules rather than discretion. But having had the advantage of a few days to think over Professor Minford's paper, it is apparent to me that the rules—as one would expect from the author—are an extremely subtle combination of long-term and short-term guidelines. I would have thought that everybody who specialises in the subject would have his own set of slightly different rules; that debates, perfectly serious debates, would be going on, amendments would be proposed to these rules, and the consensus in the economics profession, if there is one, would change slightly. Professor Minford himself might want to change one or two of these rules, and it would result in the replacement of overt discussion about fine tuning and discretion into a discussion of what the rules should be. It is very difficult to argue that one should not change the rules with increasing knowledge and experience, and yet if one does change them very much the advantages of a known framework are diminished.

This brings me to my specific worry, that the rules here are very subtle indeed. If one takes the short-term stabilisation rules, it is very interesting indeed that, if you have the kind of situation we have so often had in the last few years, of stagnation or a combination of increased inflation and increased unemployment, one rule would suggest that you should actually reduce your monetary target because of expected inflation; the other rule is that because output would be below normal you would increase the recorded PSBR. In this case you would have monetary and fiscal policy pointing in opposite directions and this would be in a long-term framework in which Professor Minford, more than some other monetarists perhaps, has emphasised that they have got to be going in the same direction, and that you cannot, in his words, finance in a non-inflationary way large PSBRs over a period. So you would need some extremely delicate sorting out of the short- and the long-term operating principles in which there would be much scope for disagreement.

I was trying to think how one would have applied them in the middle 'seventies. One of the first things one would have to know would be the natural rate of output and the natural rate of unemployment. It would be possible for two people who accept this framework of rules to disagree in some of these years. One of them might have said you have to increase the PSBR in the short term and for stabilisation reasons, and the other that you have got to reduce it. So we have quite subtle problems of interpretation, of keeping the short-term and the long-term operating rules in balance, and very considerable problems of interpretation and of asking where we are at any moment. I am suggesting that if we do need a more automatic system than we have, a lot in this table would have to be greatly elaborated.

MINFORD: First of all, the 'cosmetic cuts' as you have defined them, are not continuing cuts. The Public Sector Borrowing Requirement is a flow whereas a cosmetic cut is a temporary change in a flow. Cosmetic cuts do not continue. They are perfectly valid cuts—I mean, if one was to expect that, year in, year out, there would be a steady stream of asset sales, which obviously is not realistic, then one would view them in a very different light. If they are backed by a continuing programme to cut the PSBR in the long term, they are perfectly reasonable, valid components of a short-run transition path. In other words, if there are some cosmetic cuts which are perfectly valid in themselves, provided they are part of a transition towards a lower long-run PSBR, there is no reason to worry whether they are temporary or not, because presumably over the longer term the relevant revenue will be raised or the spending be cut to make sure that the flow reflects it permanently.

On rules and interpretation, the points Mr Brittan has raised are very important. Clearly, for people to agree on rules that would be published and not deviated from would be a very difficult process. That may be an argument for not bothering with them at all—simply go for the long term and an agreed transition path. In many ways this, if combined with greater flexibility in the goods and labour markets, might be the best one could manage. I am perfectly open to that argument. I do not think these stabilisation rules are the be-all-and-end-all of anything; they may be moderately helpful if people could reach agreement on them. The essential point is that they should reach agreement by whatever method is necessary to reach agreement, including operational criteria, such as what is a cyclical adjustment, and so on. Then, having been agreed, they would be fixed and adhered to in order to minimise the variance of government intervention in the economy, in other words, to abolish fine tuning, the discretionary element.

I am open to the argument that this would be impossible to achieve in practical terms and so it would be better to go for straightforward fixed rules. We have the technology in principle to agree. People who had the necessary models and so forth could presumably sit around a table and agree on some working definitions which could then be published and stuck to without questions of interpretation arising of the sort you have raised, where people change their minds and government constantly changes its mind and interprets loopholes, etc.

The last point you raised was the question about monetary and fiscal stabilisation. What I explicitly said was that the monetary target—the money supply growth rate—should be reduced if inflation is accelerating or prices are accelerating, while the fiscal stabilisation rules should be varied in response to output. The reason was that in this sort of model there is a strong separation between real and monetary sectors. Money is clearly a monetary phenomenon, and the fiscal balance—the balance of demand, as it were, imposed on the economy by the budget—is a real phenomenon once you take account of the fact that the budget deficit is expected on average to be in balance (it is that which creates the link with the long-run monetary target.) The point is that, provided confidence is maintained in the long-run policies for money supply growth and the PSBR, it is possible to use to modest advantage in the short run the different leverage exerted by temporary changes in them. This could mean for a time that money and the PSBR leant in 'opposite directions'; but this would not violate the underlying consistency of monetary and fiscal policy.

POSTSCRIPT
An Illustrative Set of Rules and Operational Criteria
by A. P. L. MINFORD

In response to the discussion raised by Mr Samuel Brittan, I have attempted to illustrate how these monetary and fiscal proposals would work in practice. Of course by doing so I fall into the trap that one who disagrees may find fault with the detail of the example and so damn the general proposal. However, I take my chance with such debating tactics.

A set of rules

A simple but effective set of rules would be:

1. tax *rates* (not revenues) are fixed in advance for each year.
2. the average tax rate for the following year (expressed as a percentage of GDP) is raised by x (say 0·1) per cent (e.g. from 27 to 27·1 per cent) above the target tax rate for every 1 per cent of 'excess demand' expected in the coming year, and *vice-versa*.
3. the short-run target growth for money supply in the coming year is lowered by y (say 0·1) per cent (e.g. from 10 to 9·9 per cent) for every 1 per cent of expected 'excess inflation' in the coming year, and *vice-versa*.

'Excess demand' is defined as a weighted average of available indicators including the CBI capacity utilisation index,[1] the CBI index of skilled labour shortage[1] and the general vacancy rate.[2] Because of the difficulties surrounding the interpretation of the unemployment rate, it would *not* be included. The weights should be equal unless strong reasons are given that a particular factor of production—labour, capital or any other—is a bigger constraint than others. In principle the weights should reflect these factor constraints.

'Excess inflation' is defined as the difference between the inflation rate and the long-run inflation target implied by the long-run budget deficit and money supply targets.

It is easy enough to see how this framework would work if the economy was starting from equilibrium. With a zero long-run PSBR target and 3 per cent money supply target (supposing this to be the normal growth of output), the implied inflation target is zero. Then if, due to some unexpected (e.g. oil) shock, the economy moves into recession in year 1, and is expected to remain, say, 3 per cent below potential in year 2, the government lowers the tax rate for year 2 temporarily by 0·3 per cent. If at the same time inflation of 5 per cent occurs unexpectedly in year 1 and is expected to continue at 3 per cent in year 2, government finances the resulting deficit by expanding the supply of money at only 2·7 per cent in year 2 (and issuing correspondingly more bonds to the non-bank private sector)—again temporarily. There is no contradiction between fiscal and monetary policy here, merely a *temporary* opposition of direction; money will affect mainly prices, the budget will affect mainly output.

Less easy to see is how the system would work starting from disequilibrium—e.g. from the present 'stagflation'. Say we have a PSBR of 6 per cent of GDP, inflation at 10 per cent p.a., GDP 6 per cent below potential,

---

[1] Published monthly in the CBI's *Monthly Trends Inquiry*, CBI, 21 Tothill Street, London SW1.

[2] *Source: Dept. of Employment Gazette.*

and money supply growth of 12 per cent p.a. Now there is a policy change. The 'normal' PSBR is planned to fall to 0 in 4 years, e.g. by 1·5 per cent each year, the normal money supply growth to fall to 3 per cent in 4 years, e.g. by 2¼ per cent each year. This new policy would imply some forecast profile for GDP and inflation over the coming 4 years. In so far as this implies excess supply/demand or excess inflation as defined, the *actual* PSBR and money supply targets for each year would be adjusted by the rule. So the *transition path* of budget and money supply growth would depend on the forecast for output and inflation.

Rules not immutable

These rules would be published and held to. However, they need not be permanently immutable. If the structure of the economy were to change, the stabilisation rule could appropriately change with it; but the important point is that it would be changed publicly after appropriate public debate, much as (at least in principle) the tax structure is changed.

Who would decide the appropriate rules and any change in them over time? This is a question of constitutional mechanics which I deliberately omit. On such issues I am relatively optimistic (perhaps naïvely so) that, once the *ideas* in these proposals are clearly understood, governments, with the help of Parliamentary committees, should be able to put them into practice without deception and with good will. But more formal mechanisms, if they can be implemented, would no doubt be helpful.

4. Micro-economic Controls —Disciplining the State by Pricing

ARTHUR SELDON

Editorial Director, Institute of Economic Affairs

The Author

ARTHUR SELDON: Editorial Director, IEA; formerly tutor in economics, University of London Commerce Degree Bureau, examiner in economics, London School of Economics; special adviser, Cabinet Committee on Welfare, Government of Australia, 1968; Member, BMA Committee on Health Services Financing, 1970; co-author with Ralph Harris of several IEA studies, the latest *Over-Ruled on Welfare* (June 1979); co-compiler, *Everyman's Dictionary of Economics;* author of *Charge* (Temple Smith, 1977); essay, 'Individual Liberty, Public Goods and Representative Democracy', in Hayek Festschrift, *ORDO*, No. 30, 1979.

Introducing Arthur Seldon, Lord Robbins said:

In introducing the distinguished man who is about to address you, I cannot forbear from paying tribute to what Arthur Seldon has done in the diffusion of sensible discussion about intricate economic questions, I personally think that the achievement of the IEA, whether you agree with them or disagree, is really one of the few hopeful intellectual events that have happened in the last 20 years, and certainly a great deal of credit goes to Mr Seldon.

I. INTRODUCTION

We are here to discuss the 'taming' of government because it has become 'wild'—out of control, undisciplined, inordinate.

We therefore think it can be cut down to size, be put in its place.

And if you think these descriptions are strong, I would draw your attention to a sober academic, Professor Richard Rose of the University of Strathclyde who has entitled his new book *Can Government Go Bankrupt?*.[1]

Lord Robbins and Professor Littlechild have discussed what government should do and what it should not do. There is wide—and widening—agreement that it is doing much that it should not, and, as a result, not doing very well what it should.

Professor Tullock has indicated one large reason why it has grown too fast: bureaucracy is not only a result but also a cause of growing government that has grown too far.

The conceptually simplest, quickest way to take from Caesar what is not Caesar's is to 'de-socialise' much of it: to transfer to the market fuel and transport, steel and motor-cars, much of education and medicine, all house-building, and many local services from water and ambulances, abattoirs and airports, to fire-fighting and refuse collection.

That would entail much tension and strife. It may be the ultimate solution, but if politicians shrink from the confrontation with public officials, trade unions and the advocates of big government, other methods may have to be used sooner or later. The one I would urge

---

[1] Macmillan, 1979.

—replacing taxing by charging for public services wherever possible and economic—would have the same ultimate results but might possibly avoid the confrontations because it would transfer the decisions on cutting public services from politicians to the public itself.

Professor Minford has reviewed one kind of discipline that would hold it in check: *macro*-economic controls. I now urge *micro*-controls, that is, disciplining government by subjecting it to market forces. I think we shall not be able to cut government down to size as much as is desirable *unless we put it into the market to justify itself* to the consumer—the taxpayer-citizen—in competition with any other supplier who can compete with it.

Before I do that I should say why I think macro-control, like patriotism, is not enough.

II. MACRO-CONTROLS NOT ENOUGH

My main doubt about macro-controls is that they are operated by the very people, politicians and bureaucrats, who inflated and distended government in the first place. And I fear that they will find ways round conventional macro-controls and whatever new ones are devised, however sophisticated and subtle.

Consider the constitutional/legal macro-controls proposed in recent months to discipline local government councillors and their officials.

- councils asking for rates increases exceeding 20 per cent should have to be re-elected;
- a rates referendum to approve each year's rate increase;
- strengthening the legal powers of the District Auditor (who can surcharge councillors for 'unreasonable' expenditure);
- taking councils to court for failing to provide services for which they have charged, as recently in the London borough of Haringey;
- stronger central government power to sanction loans for capital expenditure;
- rates strikes or delays;
- stricter cash limits—not only on central government grants but also on annual spending programmes and possibly rates increases; and, what the *Economist* calls 'the best hope': direct election of

mayors to represent the citizen who, it rightly implies, is not effectively championed by the councillors who are supposed to represent him.

No doubt each of these expedients would help. And together they might do a lot. But I doubt it. Even if cash limits set a ceiling to grants from central government and to payments by local government, they leave the local politicians and apparatchiks to decide which expenditure or service to cut down more and which less, and indeed which to increase within the general lower total. So we should probably end up with *less* spent on services the public wants *more,* say, police or roads, and *more* spent on services it wants *less,* perhaps overseas aid or housing subsidies. Macro-controls are clumsy, crude and indiscriminate: they are too much like a scythe that decapitates flowers as well as weeds.

[Examples were soon forthcoming. Following the cuts in expenditure ordered by the new Government, public officials, such as several Chief Education Officers, indicated they would use them to inconvenience the public in order to discredit the policy and generate opposition to it. A more extreme form of obstruction to macro-control was the refusal of an Area Health Authority in London to apply the policy. We can imagine the ingenuity public officials can apply in this process of manipulating government policy to serve their interests rather than the public. But we should be surprised: if there is criticism it is of those who expected public officials to put themselves second.—August 1979.]

III. HOW MUCH STATE SPENDING ON GENUINE PUBLIC GOODS?

Unfortunately, macro-controls are probably the only ones available for some services, national or local—the so-called 'public' goods proper—that government must supply because they cannot be refused to people who refuse to pay for them and hope to have 'free rides'. The obvious examples range from national defence to local street lighting. Taxing may therefore be the only way of paying for them, and government can control them in some fashion by cash ceilings and limits on tax revenue. Here government may be a necessary evil.

But such *jointly* consumed public goods account for only a third or so of total government expenditure. About two-thirds is spent on cash transfers and *separable* personal goods that can be refused to people who refuse to pay. Yet government goes on supplying them and taxing us to pay for them.

Table I shows the figures in a recent year. Public goods proper account for around 15 per cent of government expenditure (Group I). These are mainly external military defence, internal civil defence, Parliament itself, the law courts, public health. I must add that some American economists are examining methods of charging for even some in this category.

The rest I have divided into two groups: those which can *partly* be paid for separately by each user (Group II) and those that can *largely* or *wholly* be paid for separately (Group III). Group II, embracing mainly roads and research, police and fire services, comprises 14 per cent of government expenditure, of which I imagine about 4 per cent could be paid for separately, leaving 10 per cent to be provided out of taxes. Group III comprises 40 per cent of government expenditure. It ranges from education, housing and medicine to employment offices ('job centres'), libraries, art galleries, museums, water, sewage, refuse collection, school meals, milk, welfare foods and the oddly-named 'personal social services' like home helps and meals on wheels. Most of it can be paid for separately: the residue, I judge, would be perhaps 10 per cent to be provided by government.

Thus only 35 per cent of all government expenditure goes on public goods proper, and the rest on separable private benefits and cash payments. Since 70 per cent of government expenditure is on services and 30 per cent on cash payments, half of it is on private services that do not have to be supplied by government.

Where separate payment is possible it is the better way of disciplining government because the decision on where to control or reduce government is exercised by the individual consumer. It is therefore a more certain control or discipline on government than are macro-controls.

The mechanism is quite clear and simple: if you pay directly for something in the market you buy ('demand') less than if you pay indirectly to government through taxes, because you then think its price is nil—that it is 'free'.

There is no more effective discipline on over-spending than *knowing* the price and having to *pay* it. First, you *know* how much you pay if you pay by price; you do *not* know how much you pay if you pay in *taxes*. How many people—even in this exceptionally

TABLE I

GOVERNMENT EXPENDITURE ON PUBLIC AND PERSONAL GOODS

	Proportion of total government expenditure %	*Proportion of gross national product* %
I. Public goods with inseparable benefits (charging impracticable or uneconomic)		
Military defence	10	6
Civil defence	*	*
External relations (embassies, missions, EEC, etc.)	2	1
Parliament & law courts	1	*
Prisons	*	*
Public Health	*	*
Land drainage & coast protection	*	*
Finance & tax collection	1	1
Other government services	*	*
	15	8
II. Public goods with some separable benefits (charging partly practicable)		
Government (central & local) and 'public' corporation current & capital expenditure	6	3
Roads and public lighting	3	2
Research	1	*
Parks, pleasure grounds, etc.	1	*
Local government services ('misc.')	2	1
Police	2	1
Fire services	*	*
Records, registration, surveys	*	*
	14	8

*Less than one per cent.

73

	Proportion of total government expenditure %	Proportion of gross national product %
III. Substantially or wholly separable benefits (charging substantially practicable		
Education	12	7
National Health Service	9	5
Personal social services	2	1
School meals, milk & welfare foods	1	*
Employment service	1	*
Libraries, museums & art galleries	1	*
Housing	9	5
Water, sewage, refuse disposal	2	1
Transport & communications	5	3
	40	22
IV. Subsidies, grants, pensions and other (mostly) cash disbursements		
Agriculture, forestry, fishing, food	3	1
Cash benefits for social insurance, etc.	16	9
Miscellaneous subsidies, grants, lending, etc. to private/personal sector	3	2
	22	13
V. Interest on National Debt	9	6
TOTAL GOVERNMENT EXPENDITURE	100	56

*Less than one per cent.

---

well-informed gathering—know the cost or price of:
- a year of state schooling
- a year of state university education
- a week in hospital
- the weekly cost of providing a council house

- the cost of supplying 1,000 gallons of water or removing 1,000 gallons of sewage
- borrowing a library book
- removing a bag of refuse?

Second, paying by price requires a conscious decision to buy or not to buy; paying by tax removes the consciousness of payment.

Third, paying by price teaches care in comparing values, forethought in using money, husbandry and economy. Paying by taxes teaches none of these virtues.

Fourth, price enables you to pay for each commodity or service separately. Paying by tax for 879 or 1,253 items removes from the individual consumer the power to decide differently for each purchase —whether to spend more on one, less on another, the same on a third.

IV. CONTROLLING EXPENDITURE BY PRICING

Price is thus a more informed method of controlling expenditure and cutting government down to size: in separable personal services individuals know better than government where they want to spend their money. And where they want to spend it is largely different from where government spends it—as the results of field surveys reported in a forthcoming IEA book will indicate.[2]

V. PRICE GOVERNMENT SERVICES

Moreover, putting government into the market by charging for its services would be more likely to cut it down to size because it is politically risky for politicians to set about cutting education, health or other ostensibly 'desirable' services. Thus, although individuals would much rather spend less on state welfare (or other) services, and more on private services they can buy in the market with more choice,[3] which is what our researches over 15 years have found,

---

[2] As far as I know evidence on this proposition is provided for the first time in Britain in Ralph (now Lord) Harris & Arthur Seldon, *Over-Ruled on Welfare*, Hobart Paperback 13, IEA, 1979, Chapter 6.

[3] Evidence for this proposition has been provided since 1963 in the successive *Choice in Welfare* reports in 1963, 1965 and 1970, and finally in *Over-Ruled on Welfare*.

politicians are virtually paralysed in their role of reflecting individual public preferences.

I conclude that the only effective way to discipline government in its supply of personal services is therefore to establish machinery for 'do-it-yourself' cutting by each individual, or family or household. But, to do that, we must know costs and alternative prices. And that requires government services to be clearly marked with price-labels and to be charged for wherever possible.

VI. THE CASE FOR CHARGING

What kind of figures are likely to emerge?

Many of these personal services are provided through local government—shown for a recent year in Table III. You will see the large scope for charging—or higher charging—in the 'rate-fund' services, which are supposed to be provided wholly or largely out of the rates. But even in the 'trading services', which are supposed to pay for themselves more or less, there is wide scope for higher charging, especially for cemeteries, fishing harbours, markets, slaughterhouses and airports.

Take, for example, the London Borough of Ealing. School meals in 1977-78 cost 65p but have been charged at 25p, lately revised to 35p. School transport is 'free'—or rather costs £1 million paid by rates and taxes—in a borough 4½ miles by 2½.

Nursery schools cost £170 per annum, primary schools £400, secondary schools about £450 up to fifth forms, around £600 for sixth forms. Parents could initially pay part of these costs by topping up vouchers worth, say, ¾ of total costs. By giving parents choice between state and private schools, voucher-aided partial fees would make *all* schools more efficient, more cost-conscious, and in the end cheaper.

In Ealing council housing repairs cost £100 a year each for 20,000 homes. A charge of £50 a year to start with would bring in revenue to reduce the subsidy and/or a spirited epidemic of do-it-yourself repairs. Car parking costs about 50p a day. Charges are nil. Thus motorists are subsidised by pedestrians they may knock down. Charging for refuse collection would encourage sorting of waste into the combustible, the re-usable and the residue of disposable to be collected.

TABLE II

HOW MUCH WE PAY FOR LOCAL GOVERNMENT SERVICES BY CHARGES AND BY TAXES

	Charges etc. as % of expenditure	*Remainder paid by taxes (%)*
1. 'RATE FUND' SERVICES (CURRENT EXPENDITURE)		
Education:		
Nursery	*	100
Primary	1	99
Secondary	3	97
Special	11	89
Further:		
Polytechnics & Regional colleges	9	91
Colleges of art	8	92
Agricultural	18	82
Other major colleges, etc.	12	88
Evening institutes	19	81
Other	35	65
Teacher training	3	97
School health	1	99
Recreation & social & physical training:		
Youth	2	98
Adults, etc.	7	93
Other education services	6	94
School meals, milk, etc.	34	66
Libraries	6	94
Museums and art galleries	5	95
Health:		
Health centres	8	92
Mother/children clinics, etc.	6	94
Midwifery	1	99
Visitors	*	100
Home nursing	*	100
Vaccination & Immunisation	*	100
Ambulance	2	98

*Less than £1 million or 1 per cent.

	Charges etc. as % of expenditure	Remainder paid by taxes (%)
Prevention of illness	3	97
Family Planning	1	99
Personal social services		
Residential care	26	74
Day care—day nurseries (incl. play groups)	12	88
Community care:		
Home helps (inc. laundry)	5	95
Meals in the home	18	82
Other	2	98
Police	4	96
Fire	2	98
Justice (courts, petty sessions, probation)	2	98
Sewerage	6	94
Refuse	7	93
Baths (swimming & washing) & laundries	26	74
Land drainage, flood prevention	4	96
Smallholdings	12	88
Sea fisheries, pest control etc.	27	63
Roads:		
Highways	3	97
Public lighting	2	96
Vehicle parking	60	40
Youth employment	*	100
Sheltered employment and workshops	41	59
Environment:		
Parks & open spaces	8	92
National & countryside parks	1	99
Town & country planning	4	96
Housing other than below—2)	6	94
Public conveniences	2	98
Air pollution prevention	*	100
Other health measures	6	95
River pollution prevention	*	100
Allotments	23	77

*Less than £1 million or 1 per cent.

	Charges etc. as % of expenditure	Remainder paid by taxes (%)
Private street etc., works	51	49
Registration of births, etc.	35	65
Civil defence	1	99
Coast protection	*	100
2. HOUSING (CURRENT EXPENDITURE 'REVENUE ACCOUNT')	60	100
3. 'TRADING SERVICES'	60	40
Water	84	16
Passenger transport	84	16
Cemeteries & crematoria	35	65
Fishing harbours	61	39
Other ports & piers	88	12
Civic restaurants	88	12
Markets horticultural	39	61
others	55	45
Slaughterhouses	55	45
Aerodromes	63	37
Industrial estates	20	80
District heating schemes	83	17
Corporation estates	15	85

*Less than £1 million or 1 per cent.

And so in many other areas—for libraries, lavatories, sports centres, the police, art galleries, water, seaside beaches, even justice.

VII. THE CASE FOR HEALTH CHARGES

Not least the apparently most difficult service of all—health. I have no doubt we should have better medical care if we withdrew some of the taxes we give the apparatchiks and make them sell their personal services to us for prices, charges and fees.

Prescriptions cost on average £2. Since 1969 we have paid 20p.[4] Visits to family doctors probably cost around £3-£5: we pay directly

---

[4] Raised in June 1979 Budget to 45p—still less than one-quarter of the cost.

nothing. Hospitals can cost upward of £350 a week: we pay directly nothing.

In spite of the view that doctors influence or control the demand for their services as well as the supply, and that price has lost its power to control demand, I have little doubt that charges for family doctors would prune sub-marginal calls on their services and time; higher charges for prescriptions would reduce the amount of pills poured down bathroom basins; and charges for hospitalisation would reduce the occupancy of hospital beds by discouraging premature entry and encouraging prompt discharge, and reduce expenditure on X-ray or other investigations. If there is no price doctors and patients tend to play safe and consume resources at the expense of other uses and users.

If, as a result of NHS charges, more people went to private doctors and more private hospitals were built, the state would have to sell off—de-socialise—some hospitals. And that would cut out unnecessary government power.

VIII. OBJECTIONS REFUTED

Is it all practicable?

(1) Is it *administratively* workable?

The reply is that charging works in Europe, Australasia, North America, for health services through systems of insurance, private and governmental, voluntary and compulsory. They are by no means faultless but they are constantly studied and periodically refined.

(2) Is charging *socially* acceptable? What about the poor?

Even in health there is no insuperable difficulty. A reverse income tax in one form or other could provide the purchasing power for people with low incomes to pay charges. Their premiums could be paid for by government on a sliding scale—as has been done in Australia.

Health vouchers could enable them to shop around for health insurance that suited them, as the Secretary of State for Health, Education and Welfare in the USA has been urged to introduce.[5]

I would therefore not exempt pensioners or children as such. Many pensioners can pay and the others, except the mentally subnormal,

---

[5] By Professor Alain C. Enthoven of Stanford University, California.

could be enabled to pay. Many would prefer it that way. Many children have parents who could pay, and other parents could be enabled to pay. The same goes for nursing mothers. The criterion for paying charges or receiving free services is not age or physical or legal condition or anything else but income.

(3) Is charging *economically* realistic?

Yes—if there are large tax cuts, contracting out, reverse taxes and vouchers.

Whatever the outcome, the control of the state would decline either because the decisions to spend or not to spend on state services would lie with consumers rather than officials, or because the province of government would have been cut down.

Moreover consumer satisfaction—the efficiency of their expenditures—would increase because they would be exchanging unresponsive government services without choice for responsive private services with choice.

Not least, although demand for a service will fall as its price rises, people will willingly pay *more* for higher quality for themselves of their families. That is why people would spend more voluntarily on private education and medicine, etc. than they do compulsorily in taxes for state education and the NHS.

(4) Is charging *politically* possible?

In the absence of government attempts to discover public acceptability of charges as an alternative to paying for welfare by taxes, IEA surveys over 15 years have tried to discover the extent and trend of public attitudes and preferences. We have gone beyond simple opinion polling by introducing and emphasising price. We have asked national samples of heads of households of working age, who make these decisions, whether they would prefer to pay higher taxes for more state services or contract out, have lower taxes, but pay privately. We thus avoided the trap into which politicians and opinion-makers have fallen of asking merely if people would like lower taxes—to which the predictable reply is 'Yes'; and of asking them if they want better public services, to which the again predictable reply is 'Yes'. The public have thus been misled into contradictory replies because they have not been supplied with the missing link—price. When price is introduced, the public indicates rational, consistent choices.[6]

---

[6] *Over-Ruled on Welfare, op. cit.*

Their preference for contracting out and paying by price or charges rather than by taxes has risen for education from 47 per cent in 1963 to 77 per cent in 1978 and for medical care from 57 per cent in 1963 to 72 per cent in 1978. That trend—with variations—goes through both sexes, all ages, all socio-economic groups and all party sympathies. And it is a measure of the degree to which the absence of the market enables government to ride roughshod over public preferences.

IX. OPPONENTS OF CHARGING

There will be obstruction to the introduction of charging.

First, the demagogues will say price would damage the public services, dismantle the welfare state, weaken the fabric of government. I hope it eventually does all three. These reforms are long overdue. Government in Britain has passed out of public control; it has become wild, and it is high time it was tamed.

But charging would destroy only the so-called 'public' services that government *should not supply at all* because they can be supplied in the market. It would dismantle *state* welfare but probably strengthen the welfare services as such by changing their suppliers from a public monopoly to state and private competitors. And it would weaken only *unnecessary* government. It would in time strengthen the residue of necessary government by leaving it supplying public goods proper.

Second, the trade unions will obstruct charging. Possibly only a change in the law will stop them.

Third, the bureaucrats will obstruct charging. We shall have to retire them early, transfer some to the industry market, buy them out, or ignore them. I leave them to Professor Rowley (Paper 6, pp. 107-123).

Fourth, many academics will obstruct charging. Even good economists have neglected an instrument—the pricing system—their profession has spent two centuries refining and perfecting. I must say I am surprised how few economists indicate the relevance of pricing in all the discussion of government expenditure and how to control it.

X. DRAWBACKS OF CHARGING

Charging has drawbacks, mainly four:

(i) It may be more costly to administer than a system of non-charging for free goods.

(ii) Supplying some goods free may be a simple way of equalising incomes.

(iii) Few goods are entirely private: most also have effects on others, so that if charging reduces demand the 'external' good they do to others is also reduced.

(iv) There are sometimes technical difficulties in arriving at the right charge.

But there are other ways of dealing with these drawbacks, mainly by redistributing purchasing power. And even if charging is sometimes not as cheap or as certain as taxing, the drawbacks of not charging are even more damaging. These are the 'externalities' of not charging that, here again, seem strangely to be ignored, even by some economists, and especially by economists who favour state provision of services and financing them by taxes. I list ten:

1. The strain in the body politic of trying to ration resources for private services without the assistance of pricing; the result is often not scientifically ideal but politically expedient.

2. Resources are used to satisfy articulate pressure groups rather than inarticulate individuals.

3. Neglect of the services that only government can perform—not least, defence and law and order.

4. Tax-financed services usually restrict choice.

5. Government services are normally not as good at innovation as private services.

6. The high taxation required to finance 'free' goods weakens incentives to produce.

7. The tax-gatherers represent a waste of manpower.

8. High taxation incites tax avoidance and evasion, and a growing disrespect for law.

9. Government services supplied free interpose themselves between parents and children and weaken the family.

10. High taxes have lost Britain talent in science, technology, research, medicine, scholarship, engineering, the arts and sport.

I continue to wonder why economists who are technically sophisticated in identifying externalities that create market failure do not see externalities that go to the roots of the social order.

So to discipline and tame government I propose charging for

everything wherever practicable as a necessary and urgent control—with large tax cuts to make it possible.

I think we are in for a very interesting, exciting, perhaps abrasive, but hopeful ten years.

Questions and Discussion

PROF. CEDRIC SANDFORD (*University of Bath*): I have two comments. First, in the list of government expenditures it would be appropriate to include what the Americans call tax expenditures, i.e. particularly the relief of incentive under the tax system which might be eliminated to make possible lower rates of tax. For example, housing, where taxes ought to take housing relief into account. Second, when one is looking at the external effects—the disadvantages—of taxation financed services, one ought to take into account the compliance cost of taxation as well as the administrative cost—i.e. the costs imposed on the individual taxpayer in complying with the requirements of the tax code, both personal taxpayers and third parties like firms that have to administer a VAT scheme, for example.

SELDON: Have you estimated your two items?

SANDFORD: Not really, but we're in the process of doing so.

OLIVER STUTCHBURY: While I am wholly in sympathy with practically everything Mr Seldon has said, as someone who lives in the country I am continually astonished that, despite refuse disposal alleged to be free, people seem to prefer at huge expense to drive up in their cars and tip all their refuse on to my land. Farmers generally find this, too, and I wonder, if people were charged for refuse disposal, whether it would not be even worse. And what would you do to compensate us?

SELDON: There is a common law which protects you by a right of action with damages.

STUTCHBURY: But what would the cost be to keep somebody watching the whole time?

R. C. SANSOM: May I suggest that Mr Stutchbury charges a very high rate for putting the stuff on his land and then they won't do it any longer.

J. D. G. WATHEN (*Barclays Bank*): I must say the best way of keeping awake after lunch is to listen to Mr Seldon. Really what we are talking about here is politics. How are these ideas going to get through to the politicians?

SELDON: To some extent they are 'got over' by dissemination and education. They have not yet come out in public policies, but they are in a number of public minds.

LORD ROBBINS: I take it that if you were confronted with the question of what to do with extreme poverty coupled with misfortune of one kind or another, or even extreme poverty coupled with perhaps inherited inability to earn enough to make a living, your answer would be, as I think my answer would be—capitulating a lot to most of what you have said—that your proposals would be much more acceptable if they were coupled with some sort of negative income tax?

SELDON: I thought I had said that. Yes, I assume a system of income supplementation by a reverse income tax. In our two main government services, education and health, merely supplying money would probably not, for a period, create a redirection of demand, so I would, for a period at least, use a system of vouchers for schools and medicine. But I would use quite a wide battery of devices. In America, in Australia, in Canada, economists are discussing all sorts of exciting new techniques like tax credits and so on. Somehow in England our welfare state seems to have deadened the interest of some economists in techniques of this kind. But side by side, and even possibly as a first step, we should go in for a system of supplementation of low incomes. Both the parties have discussed variants of supplementation: Labour was talking about a minimum income guarantee in 1966, and the Conservatives had worked on a system of tax credits in 1972.

DR RALPH HORWITZ (*London Regional Management Centre*): I am interested in the relationship, almost the theoretical relationship, of the micro-economic to the macro-economic. As I understand it, the macro-economic position is that what Mr Seldon is proposing, which is a method, does not alter the macro-economic magnitudes, because you are really dealing with transfers or transfer arrangements. If, instead of spending my money on gambling or drinking, I have as a first priority of income decision to spend it on health or education, is there not a presumption that the macro-economic magnitudes would indeed change and that, quite apart from the arguments you have advanced, it would significantly alter the macro-economic totals and not simply the methods of payment?

SELDON: If demands were inelastic a system of charging would bring more revenue into the government for its use. My hunch would be that a system of charging for, say, state health services would in time bring about a shift of demand to private services if people are going to have to pay for services which have been for 30 years either wholly or partly free. By charging for state services you are in effect 'reducing' the price of private services. And that in time would lead to a diversion of demand.

85

People would say: if I have to pay for the state hospital I might as well add a bit, buy health insurance and use private hospitals which offer me a choice, and which will also save me time since they will do my hernia or varicose veins sooner and at a time to suit me. By the law of demand, if you have a higher price for state services you would have a lower demand; and people in time would shift outside the area of the state. The macro quantities would therefore go down.

C. M. JACKSON (*Spillers*): May I make one observation and ask two questions? The observation is that my company happens to own a number of slaughterhouses and I notice Table 2 under Trading Services records a significant amount of public funds going to slaughterhouses, an industry in which there is considerable over-capacity. And the privately-owned companies are finding profitability difficult because of the public funds going into the public sector.

The first question is—following up Lord Robbins's observation—what happens when somebody who is very poor has a period of prolonged illness? Second, we are coming up to an election now: how soon are we going to have the papers from this Seminar so that we can see the detail of all the fascinating observations that have been made during it?

SELDON: We hope we can publish the papers—and your questions and so on—fairly quickly, but not by 3 May. If prolonged illness—which, I should add, is rare—were not incurable, the state might have to pay, but it would not necessarily supply the services itself.

LORD ROBBINS: You must buy Mr Seldon's book called *Charge*, which is now on sale, unless stocks are exhausted.

SELDON: On subsidised slaughterhouses: if there were higher charges, indeed if there were economic charges for local authority services, I presume butchers would use your services rather than the less efficient ones run by local government.

CHRISTOPHER MEAKIN: This absurd distinction between the 'politically possible' and what it is variously contrasted with: the practical, the sensible, the desirable, or the attainable. Since Bennery, a combination of the absurd and the unattainable, has been foisted upon us by the simple expedient of repeating it over and over and over again, Mr Seldon stands a far better chance with his basically sensible proposition. It simply requires repeated repetition. The IEA has done it magnificently. There is a tremendous risk of defeatism among the radical anti-socialist right, having been in the minority for so long, though probably on the verge of becoming a majority now, to be unable to believe that these ideas can indeed become normality. Now the key to making them politically possible and practical is to talk about them and their alternative ideas. This is why I suspect Mr Seldon really had a double purpose in entitling his book *Charge*.

R. C. SANSOM: If your most ambitious thoughts were realised, what might this mean either in terms of percentage of government and local expenditure, or converting to a rough taxation percentage?

SELDON: I said that in Table 1 I calculated that about two-thirds of all government expenditure, or half of expenditure on services were not public goods, i.e. they were those for which you could charge—in time. If government expenditure is now something over half of GNP, or about £60 billion, including cash transfers, which account for about a fifth of government outlays, you would get something like £25 billion. It might take more than a year or two but there is something like that volume of goods and services now supplied by government which could eventually be transferred to charging. By waiting for people to make their own choices, and in time deciding whether or not to continue to pay for government services or to go outside the state, you could in time shift a massive amount of 'public' private expenditure outside the state—something of the order of a fifth of GNP.

SANSOM: Half of total government expenditure?

SELDON: Yes.

SANSOM: Are you sure? 25 out of 60?

SELDON: That's right. That would include a large part of the National Health Service, all of housing, a lot of local government, or most of it, and a lot of small services. I see no reason at all for any local authority to supply public libraries. I can see a case for it supplying a degree of purchasing power for people with low incomes; but I can see no reason for public or local authority-owned 'shops' which lend books.

C. M. JACKSON: Leaving aside the question of whether any absolute economies result or not, this represents a zone of potentially much greater choice.

CECIL MARGOLIS (*C. Margolis (Harrogate) Ltd.*): Four years ago I suggested that certain places were needed for car parks in the Yorkshire Moors and should be charged for. The idea was then turned down by the County Council. But last year it was adopted, they purchased an honesty box for £49, and within the year the Council collected £500 in car-parking charges. This is an example of where the rates were helped by charging. We had to lay an asphalt base which the rates would have had to finance. But now we do not need to support it any more because it is more than self-supporting. Incidentally, there have been no complaints from the public about the charge.

PROF. CHARLES ROWLEY: Somebody raised a question which to many people might be worrying: it related specifically to health. Where the individual's demand for a particular commodity may be unforeseen because it may vary considerably, contingent on unpredictable health conditions, it might be seen as a detriment to the scheme that suddenly he would have to face heavy health charges. A market solution would almost certainly be of an insurance variety; by pooling resources the contingent liabilities would be met by the insurance company. That would enable individual doctors and hospitals to charge and the insurance companies would pay.

SELDON: American health insurers have shown that the costs of insuring for catastrophic health risks, which if they occur to you are massive, and will ruin you if you are not insured, are quite low. It is a very small chance of a large risk, but it entails a low cost.

GORDON RICHARDS (*Hammersmith & West London College of Further Education*): One can be forgiven a certain amount of pessimism, when one reads the Shadow Education Secretary's statement two days ago promising higher grants for university and polytechnic students. As a quondam politician myself, now going straight, I can understand the dilemma on the eve of an election because he is speaking directly to his political constituency, the middle class whose children benefit very much from higher education. It is going to take a great deal of determination on the part of a Conservative government to tell middle-class parents that in future they really ought to be paying much more for their children's education, because it is being provided at the expense of the working class who get very little out of it.

LORD ROBBINS: There is a solution to that problem, namely, the scheme put forward by Professor Alan Prest, whereby funds should be available to all who satisfy entrance admission requirements to polytechnics and universities but if subsequent income passes a certain point the loan should be amortised through the machinery of the Inland Revenue. This solves the problem of the very clever girl who decides that her function in life is to bring up a family rather than to be a doctor or a lawyer. She is no longer laden with a negative dowry. If you had a straightforward loan scheme, it would solve the problem of the student suddenly afflicted or endowed with piety who decides to take a curacy rather than a high-paid job. Prest's scheme is I think altogether admirable; it solves the distributive problem of grants on the one hand and loans on the other.

A. F. G. SCANLAN (*BP Oil*): I would like to switch back to the difficulties of starting with micro-economic examples as indicators of how to do without macro-policies. Ealing is the borough in which I have lived for the last 20 years. What you did not mention on schooling is that the 'bussing' was brought in because of the language problem: immigrants had 8,000 children who did not speak English, mostly living in the West end, or it used to be Southall. They are bussed across the six miles to break up the language barrier. The cost-benefit analysis of that position in the light of that information might look a little different. Secondly, on car parking: Ealing was under planning blight for 15 years without an agreed new scheme. Everybody, including my wife, was shopping at Wembley, and the car parking has brought back to Ealing traders far more than the subsidy in the past. Examples are treacherous things!

SELDON: I can see a case for bussing in areas like that where you want to encourage mixing—although there is a case against that kind of mixing. What I do not see is that the buses have to be supplied free. Are all those parents of low income? Must they all be subsidised by other ratepayers, some of whose incomes may be even lower?

SCANLAN: They are first stop off from Bombay. These are the impoverished Asians coming into London.

SELDON: Then when their incomes have risen you can start charging. On car parking: I am glad you asked that, because this is atypical—it is an archetype. You can always find external benefits for everything—car parks, free libraries, . . . there is nothing that does *no* external good. There is no end to this argument: you can justify the extreme socialisation of everything on the ground that everything will do some good somewhere.

LORD ROBBINS: Arthur has taken the initiative in brevity. I call on Dr Budd to explain to us the fascinating problem of disarming the Treasury.

5. Disarming the Treasury

ALAN BUDD*

London Graduate School of Business Studies

*I am grateful to my colleagues at the London Business School for helpful comments on an earlier draft.

The Author

ALAN BUDD: Williams and Glyn's Research Fellow in Banking, London Graduate School of Business Studies, since 1974. Universities of Southampton, 1966-69, and Carnegie-Mellon, 1969-70. Senior Economic Adviser, Treasury, 1970-74. Editor, *Economic Outlook;* author of *The Politics of Economic Planning* (1978).

Introducing Dr Budd, Lord Robbins said:

I must say, just by way of preliminary, that I am always a little perplexed when people use the term 'the Treasury', and I am quite sure that Dr Budd will be able to remove my perplexity at once. A great many people are of the opinion that the Treasury manages the tax system of this country, whereas, in point of fact, the tax system is managed by the Inland Revenue and the Department of Customs and Excise, the heads of each of which have direct access to the Chancellor. I myself have been present at a sub-committee of the famous Budget Committee in which the head of the Treasury has simply said: 'We must not discuss that unless Sir Cornelius Gray [then head of the Inland Revenue, now dead— he was a very good man] is present'. The Inland Revenue and Customs and Excise are separate sovereign states in this hierarchy of Whitehall, so perhaps you would explain to us whom you are going to disarm. Or are you going to disarm the lot?

I. INTRODUCTION

It is the Treasury that I plan to disarm, although of course I am aware of the constitutional position of the Inland Revenue and Customs & Excise. I have been involved in these battles myself. It is laid down that in the end the Treasury has the final word on matters of budgetary policy, and the Inland Revenue and Customs & Excise have the final word on questions of administration of the tax system. But I was at any rate going to say, by way of introduction, how this paper fits in with the rest of the Seminar.

I take it that the expression 'the taming of government' includes the taming of the Civil Service. Professor Tullock told you this morning how desirable that would be, and it seemed to me that at the same time he told us how quite impossible it would be. My object of interest is the Treasury. I am not going to argue that it should be abolished or even necessarily reduced in size, although I may believe that one or other of those, if not both, would be a good idea. The reason I am interested in the Treasury is that for most of the post-war period the Treasury has epitomised the interventionist approach to economic policy. I happen to believe that that interventionist approach has been mistaken. It has persistently promised

93

more than it can achieve, and the end-result of intervention—and you yourself mentioned this in your opening remarks, my Lord Chairman—has usually been ever-rising inflation and a yet more structurally unbalanced economy. And for those reasons I would most gladly see the economic role of government much reduced. That view has been well covered both at the micro-economic and the macro-economic level in previous papers.

I want to concentrate on one aspect of the Treasury's role. It is the Treasury's job to advise the Chancellor on economic policy. I do not question its duty to perform that task but I do question the way it carries it out. I think it undesirable that the Treasury has been able to play such a crucial part in the formulation of economic policy. My main criticism is that the Treasury has become the primary and virtually exclusive source of official government opinion on economic matters. I believe this is undesirable, whether one takes the strong view that demand management—to take a prime example of Treasury activity—has been a dangerous delusion, or whether one merely recognises that the Treasury will occasionally be mistaken. I shall describe how the present position came about, explain why I think it is harmful, and suggest ways of remedying it.

II. THE TREASURY'S ECONOMIC ROLE

I shall concentrate on demand management, since this is the key to the Treasury's post-war development and has become the area in which its position is most strongly entrenched. The modern system of demand management through the use of fiscal policy was invented by the British and first applied by the Treasury. Its acceptance—in the early years of the Second World War—followed from the presence of Keynes and a brilliant group of economists in Whitehall. In those pioneer days, officials had to develop the techniques of demand management and also had to persuade Ministers of the value of the new approach to economic policy. Thus began a tradition whereby the Treasury not only took responsibility for the execution of macro-economic policy but also became an independent source of advice on economic matters. The tradition has developed to the point where the Treasury regards itself as virtually self-sufficient in the discussion of economics. It is as if the Department of Health and

Social Security relied entirely on its own resources not only for the formulation of health policy (whatever that may be) but also for medical research.

After an auspicious start both demand management and the Treasury moved into the background for a time, but the general pattern was set. The Treasury accepted responsibility for managing the general level of demand in the economy and set out to develop the necessary techniques of economic management.

Techniques of demand management

The techniques developed in Whitehall included economic forecasting. Although there had been earlier attempts at forecasting aggregate demand (including exercises by Keynes), the first serious efforts were made by officials during the war. In the early days forecasting could hardly be distinguished from national income accounting and both were developed together. The forecasting element was fairly primitive. Keynes himself was no supporter of elaborate forecasting procedures. (He had commented that an earlier exercise to forecast unemployment trends during the next few years should involve 'not . . . above a quarter of an hour's honest work for a genuine economist'.)[1]

What began through necessity has continued through custom. The Treasury has continued to conduct its own economic analysis and forecasting. For most of the post-war period, the activity was fairly modest. Few were involved full time in economic forecasting, although a large cast (in the Treasury and other economic departments) was assembled for the major exercises. Research was a part-time activity, although there was a brief and fruitful period in the early 'sixties when the National Institute of Economic and Social Research (NIESR) operated in effect as the Treasury's research department. The major shift occurred from the mid-sixties onwards when the Labour Government made extravagant claims for its ability to improve the performance of the economy. A large number of economists was recruited for the task. Ironically it was at about that time that the factors which had sustained the British economy since the war were ending. The limitations of demand management were soon to be starkly revealed.

---

[1] Quoted in S. Howson and D. Winch, *The Economic Advisory Council, 1930-1939*, Cambridge University Press, 1977, p. 135.

Secrecy: to protect the State or the executive?

Although the Treasury's monopoly of economic advice was initiated by the fact that Whitehall pioneered the ideas and techniques of demand management, it has been most strongly sustained by the Treasury's tradition of secrecy. It is worth recalling that there are two separate functions for secrecy in government, though it often suits Whitehall's case to confuse them. First, secrecy protects the state; second, it protects the executive. In the first function, the question of national security hardly arises in economic management; the main concern is to prevent anyone, friend or foe, from gaining an unfair advantage through prior knowledge of policy change. (That concern, incidentally, is usually relied on to prevent the open discussion of policy changes; it is worth asking whether it should not instead determine the range of policy options.) Unfortunately the principle of security under this heading is very widely defined, since it is argued that almost any discussion of economic policy gives a clue to the Government's intentions.

It is the second function of secrecy—that of protecting the executive—which is the more worrying. The constitutional principle is that officials give advice in confidence to Ministers who accept public responsibility for the resulting decisions. This principle virtually rules out the public discussion of policy matters by civil servants. There may be freedom to discuss technical issues, but the boundary in economics between technical and political issues is ill-defined, and there are ever-present risks of straying into questions that involve ministerial responsibility. If officials do discuss such questions they only defend policy decisions. The result is that economists working in Whitehall are constrained in public discussion not because of the intrinsic nature of their work but because they are civil servants. This has had a dual effect in reinforcing Whitehall's monopoly. First, the tradition of secrecy has led to a preference for hiring economists to work in the Treasury rather than using outside economists. Secondly, it has greatly reduced the incentive for outsiders to take an interest in questions of macro-economics. Whitehall argues that it has to do its own macro-economics because no-one else is interested, but it fails to recognise that it has killed that interest by its own exclusiveness.

III. THE COSTS OF MONOPOLY: MYSTIQUE AND MYTH

The Treasury's responsibility as the ultimate provider of advice to the Chancellor is not in question. The dangers arise from the control it exercises over the policy debate through its position as an exclusive and self-sufficient source of economic analysis. The Treasury, isolated from outside views, can give mistaken advice and is liable to stick to it long after its error should have been recognised. Outsiders are, of course, just as likely to make mistakes, but the Treasury will be particularly prone to accept and defend certain kinds of policies.

If a large group of people has been assembled to manage the economy, it is unlikely to decide that the economy does not need managing. Armed with the instruments of demand management and encouraged by a forecasting system which shows how effective demand management can be, the Treasury will assume that the economy cannot be trusted to run itself. When the mystique of forecasting is combined with the myth of demand management, the value of market forces will seem trivial indeed against the power of fiscal policy.

When demand management comes under attack, the immediate response is to defend current policies, because the Treasury's job is not only to give advice but also to defend Ministers' decisions based on that advice. The defence of ministerial decisions (through the provision of briefing papers) is an accepted part of the official's job, and will be done even if the official has reservations about the policy; but there is a danger that the Treasury's efforts will also be devoted to the defence of its own official views. In other words, the Treasury can become so identified with a policy that it takes on some of the qualities of a Party and questions of loyalty and the presentation of a united front become more important than the disinterested pursuit of truth. Such behaviour is, of course, not unknown among academics and in independent institutions; but at least there is more scope for diverse views between competing groups.

Secrecy hinders communication

The combination of secrecy and group loyalty produces a peculiar form of communication between outsiders and the Treasury. ('Dialogue' is certainly *not* the correct description). Outsiders give advice to the Treasury in much the same way that a newcomer to the district leaves his card at the Great House. Whether it is thrown

97

on the fire or borne rapidly to the mistress's boudoir may depend on the nature of the message or even on the whim of the butler. The outsider does not know the grounds on which his advice is ignored or discussed, and is unlikely to know why or whether it has been accepted or rejected. He fights on completely unequal terms with the officials.

To be fair, I should mention that my Treasury friends take the opposite view. They argue that it is they who suffer from the practice of giving their advice in secret. Their views are thus readily swept aside by outside academic and journalistic critics, whose own views receive far more attention from Ministers and the public than they deserve. I happen to think they are wrong, but even if they are right this is equally unsatisfactory, since we know nothing about the grounds on which one view rather than another is accepted.

Economic forecasting and the Treasury monopoly

The final aspect of the Treasury's role which I find worrying is its emphasis on its own economic forecasting. In a recent interview[2] Mr Healey commented on the weight attached to forecasts in policy making. As I mentioned earlier, the Treasury had to develop forecasting techniques before and after the war because no one else was doing it. In spite of the growth of forecasting in other institutions, the Treasury has retained a dominant role. It spends almost twice as much on forecasting as the NIESR and the London Business School put together.[3] The Chancellor reported that a recent study showed that the Treasury's forecasts were slightly more accurate than those of the other institutions. If that result is accepted (and such comparisons are notoriously unreliable), it may seem rather a poor return for so much extra expenditure. But the important point is that the Treasury's own forecast is bound to receive a disproportionate amount of attention, and this applies not only to the forecasts themselves but also to the ideas embodied in the model.

The most glaring illustration of the dangers of the Treasury's monopoly was the period in the early 'seventies when the Treasury, buoyed up by its economic model, persisted with an ever more

---

[2] *The Guardian*, 15 February 1979.

[3] Committee on Policy Optimisation, *Report*, Cmnd. 7184, HMSO, 1978, para. 152.

extreme version of its post-war orthodoxy in spite of the growing voice of dissent amongst academics and economic commentators.

IV. WHAT CAN BE DONE?

The Chancellor of the Exchequer requires advice on economic policy and the Treasury must be able to provide it. I have suggested that there are serious dangers in the current arrangement whereby the Treasury has tended to become an exclusive source for the Government's possible views on economic questions. In an hierarchical organisation staffed by career civil servants it is too much to hope that the debate will be broad enough. I believe that the Treasury should recognise that its task is to provide a secretariat for ensuring that the Chancellor receives advice based on expert opinion from *all* sources. This would not exclude the Treasury from offering independent advice, based on its own analysis and forecasts; but its status in providing such advice would be subsidiary to its role as a secretariat.

It may be said that a strong Chancellor can achieve the same result without any need to change the organisation. But there are considerable difficulties under the present system. 'Kitchen cabinets', for example, are seen as a threat to officials and, lacking a secretariat, are readily swept aside by the weight of the official machine. (The 'Think Tank', for similar reasons, was unable to rival the Treasury's power in macro-economic policy and soon gave up trying to do so.)

A strong Chancellor can, without doubt, ignore the Treasury's views and impose on it policies with which it disagrees. But all this is seen in terms of struggle and defeat. It is only seen in those terms because the Treasury—as a set of officials—has become identified with *one* set of views. A weak Chancellor will no doubt rely more on Treasury advice than does a strong Chancellor, but in neither case should it be the Treasury's job to develop and fight for its own line of policy.

Pressure group or secretariat?

The Treasury should be re-organised to perform the role of a secretariat rather than, as at present, the role of a pressure group. It should be able to brief the Chancellor in the light of outside as well as inside analysis. The task of marshalling opinions (including economic forecasts) should be organised systematically and should not depend on chance combinations of contacts at official or ministerial level or the outsider's ability to attract press coverage.

I propose the following form of organisation. The Policy Co-ordination Committee would be, as at present, at the centre of all official policy discussion in the Treasury.[4] It would be served by a Policy Co-ordination Unit which would draw on two sources:

(i) An External Co-ordination Unit which would organise and assess external views.

(ii) An Economic Analysis Unit which would be based on in-house analysis. The Policy Co-ordination Unit (which might have some external membership) would not be a pressure group for internal views but would base its advice on internal and external sources.

The External Co-ordination Unit would be organised to perform the following tasks:

(i) Issues. One division would be concerned with identifying policy issues in, for example, macro-economics, micro-economics, energy, etc.

(ii) Institutions. Another division would provide the link with Universities, forecasting institutions, research establishments, overseas organisations, etc.

(iii) Panels. A third division would arrange hearings and seminars.

The External Co-ordination Unit would both investigate and use the regular reports of outside institutions but would also sponsor economic research directly concerned with policy issues.

The objective, in short, is to widen considerably the sources of advice for the Chancellor (even if in the end the Treasury has to choose between them) and to reduce the weight placed on the Treasury's internally-generated views.

The Treasury model: its pitfalls

A concrete example of what is wrong with the present system and of how it might be improved is the activity with which I am most familiar, namely forecasting and model building, to which the

---

[4] An account of the current organisation of the Treasury is provided in Chapter 3 of the Report of the Committee on Policy Optimisation, *ibid.*

Treasury devotes considerable resources. Recently, under the provisions of the Industry Act, the Treasury has been required to make its model available for outside users and to publish more complete forecasts. I do not believe that either change has produced the slightest benefit to the management of the economy. The publication of the model, welcome as it may be, has not improved the standard of debate about economic policy. So far it has profited one or two entrepreneurs who were saved the trouble of building their own models, and it has introduced a new kind of awkward parliamentary question. It has encouraged the erroneous impression that study of the Treasury's model will enable outsiders to guess the Government's policy intentions. It has allowed inexperienced users to produce miraculous scenarios based on a misunderstanding of the nature and possibilities of economic models and has distracted attention from serious policy analysis.

The publication of forecasts has resulted, as happened last November, in the presentation of a set of numbers which bore no relation to those used internally for policy decisions. Even if the numbers were genuine, they are published after the relevant policy decisions have been taken so that discussion is virtually useless.[5]

V. CONCLUSION

Need for varied sources of advice

If the Government wants alternative views of how the economy works, it will not achieve this aim by allowing more people to play with the Treasury's model. It needs to ask outside bodies, including forecasters and model-builders, specific questions. This needs to be done systematically and with considerable forethought if it is to achieve useful results. Advice on any issue should be sought from a variety of institutions. It would be wrong for the Treasury to develop strong links with one external source. That source would soon in effect become part of the Treasury and subject to all the difficulties I have listed.

The usual response in recent years when the Treasury's technical proficiency has been attacked has been to pour more resources into

---

[5] For a few years after the war, economic forecasts were published in the *Economic Survey* in advance of the Budget.

the Treasury. I would suggest that this response has been mistaken and has been derived from the false belief that the Treasury should be self-sufficient. What is needed, I believe, is to reduce the weight given to the Treasury's own views, and to re-organise it so that it meets its advisory task by co-ordinating the widest possible range of opinion. It should encourage this range of opinion by providing resources, if need be, but most importantly it should show that it wants to hear what other people have to say.

Questions and Discussion

LORD ROBBINS (*Chairman*): I wonder if I might begin with one or two questions. First, would you agree that in the last analysis it is a choice between one ministerial responsibility or a number? We have models for this in the shape of the ministerial responsibilities you have been describing on the one side and on the other the American system where different departments put forward their proposals for policy. And how it comes out in the wash in Congress is anybody's guess. I think this is a most frightfully difficult question.

I have been on both sides—I have been Chairman of a newspaper where naturally of course the principles were the maximum information that could legitimately be obtained and the infamy of unnecessary secrecy, and I have also been a public servant where some secrecy seemed desirable. Both points of view are, I think, defensible.

I would like to get your reaction to this query about your own suggestion. My experience in government service, now a quarter of a century or more old and perhaps completely irrelevant, was that unless one was working definitely for a Minister with responsibility, one might just as well be not working at all. At the beginning of the Second World War a man, now dead, who was Second Secretary of the Cabinet Office, gathered together a miscellaneous collection of statisticians and economists supplementary to the Three Wise Men who were supposed to be advising the Chamberlain government. And there we all were, writing academic papers which were perhaps read in private offices but, I am quite sure, never reached Ministers. It was only when we came under the Lord President of the Council, Sir John Anderson, the economic co-ordinator during the critical part of the war (the Treasury was in the doghouse then) that one felt that what one tried to do had any meaning at all. And when I heard in 1964 that the Government had for personal reasons created the Department of Economic Affairs I thought to myself either it will need the closest possible co-operation with the Treasury, so that in effect they are one department, or it will fall away. More recently, I had exactly the same feeling about the 'Think Tank'. It was responsible to the Prime Minister, but we all know that Prime Ministers have much too much to do other than to think—let alone look after other people's thinking.

I come back to this point, that either you have, as in Britain, a Minister who is ultimately responsible to the Cabinet, or you do not. I do not really believe Professor Tullock's thesis about the enormous influence of bureaucrats in this country, though I am sure bureaucrats matter and that there is a problem there. But in the end it is the Minister who counts. Civil servants, it is true, argue with Ministers. But when a Minister has said 'I want this rather than that', it is the tradition in this country, as you know, that the superior administrative grade people do their best to make the best of what they may privately think to be a bad job. So are we to favour the American system or the single Minister system? And if the single Minister system is the more orderly, can it be other than the Treasury?

BUDD: So far as the ministerial framework is concerned, I had assumed that it was unchanged—in other words, it is not a diversity of departments on American lines. There is a slightly separate issue about the Americans: they have the institution of the Council of Economic Advisers, providing an independent source of advice to the President, but again within the British system it could only be located in the Treasury if anywhere. One could not set it up separately. A crucial point about the Chancellor, as we know very well, is that he is an extremely powerful Minister. The Chancellor acting in conjunction with the Prime Minister is absolutely invincible. Part of that power arises through secrecy. When forecasts are secret, they are secret from other Ministers. The Chancellor can stand there and say: 'We have to do the following because of something I can see on my piece of paper but I cannot tell you what it is so you will have to go along with me'. One hears of the frustration of other Ministers at that stage, so that does make the Chancellor extremely powerful.

Now I assume—since certainly what I want is more openness of debate —that inevitably the type of process I am discussing would make it more apparent to other Ministers that there was a much wider range of views about what should be done than that which the Chancellor was putting forward in Cabinet. And to this extent I can see that it would weaken the Chancellor *vis-à-vis* his Cabinet colleagues. I personally would not mind that. But I am assuming in other ways a continuation of the present constitutional arrangements.

PROF. C. K. ROWLEY (*University of Newcastle-upon-Tyne*): In the event that such a re-organisation of the Treasury took place and the Government—or the Treasury itself—was in a position to obtain information from various quarters, would you go so far as to have the Budget allocated, if you like, to the Secretariat, who could then buy in the resources for the

Treasury, or buy out into the London Business School or Cambridge or Southampton, or wherever else the forecasting facilities were, moving your economists and your advisory groups into temporary posted positions so that they were hired for a four- or five-year period, so that if the public forecasting sector was not as efficient as the London Business School, the contract would be terminated and they would have to look elsewhere for employment? Would you see that kind of market mechanism being introduced into that Department?

BUDD: It is an implication that one might hive off some of the economic services provided within the Treasury.

R. C. SANSOM: Is it not implicit in your theory that to dilute rather than disarm (I think that is the phrase I would use here), the Treasury forecast with others would necessarily represent an improvement? Speaking as a layman and not an economist, it seems to me to be arguable that it might be even more disastrous than the present arrangement. If you compare one forecast with another and with the outcomes, you might be just as well off putting your hand in a barrel in a blacked-out room. Should your theory not go on to cover the possibility—I am perhaps only saying this semi-seriously—that you might be better off with no forecasting at all, or with a purely random machine? It does seem to me your argument is that more is better, but more may be worse.

BUDD: I discussed forecasting because that is what I happen to do, but if forecasting is a waste of time the Chancellor ought to know that it is a waste of time. If providing him with more forecasts convinces him that it is a waste of time, then I am perfectly satisfied with that outcome, and the policy can then be based less on forecasting than it is currently. I would not regard that as an undesirable outcome.

PROF. D. R. MYDDELTON (*Cranfield School of Management*): I think I may have misinterpreted the title. When I think of weapons at the Treasury's disposal, I think of things like exchange controls and taxes and price controls—and you did not talk about them at all. Are you content to leave those weapons in the Treasury's power?

BUDD: I will accept the offence under the Trade Descriptions Act as far as the title of the paper is concerned. I am sure my views on exchange control and most of those other types of intervention would be very close to those presented by previous speakers, and I would hope that the type of exercise and the re-organisation of the Treasury that I am proposing would reveal the case against them.

A. F. G. SCANLAN (*BP Oil*): Could you say a word about where you see the extension of Treasury advice if it became a secretariat for the collation and coordination of outside advice?

I work in international industry where one of the things that we are concerned by is that if you take the US view of GNP you get 4 per cent growth and if you take the European view you get about 2 per cent. This must be quite a problem for any Treasury. How much weight would you give the internationalisation of advice as opposed to linking up with internal bureaux, various regional institutions, and so on?

BUDD: This would certainly be included, and one would obtain the best advice one could. This would be the notion of a market for advice. One certainly would not wish to limit it to British institutions.

SCANLAN: Are you saying that we are perhaps too inward-looking, and that the external analysis and international factors are perhaps being ignored?

BUDD: I do think the Treasury is too inward-looking. I have no doubt that is true also of British academic life. But if one compared the wider debate about economic policy in the 'seventies, which was such a crucial period for all of this, the English economists said most of the things that needed to be said. *The problem was that the Treasury did not say them.*

LORD ROBBINS: You really blame the Treasury for—so to speak—throwing the reins over the horse's head in the early 'seventies? My firmly held belief is that the responsibility was Ted Heath's.

BUDD: This matter is covered by requirements of secrecy and so on, and since I was there at the time it is slightly hard for me to talk about it. I can think of the one just man, or possibly the two just men, who were there in that Sodom and Gomorrah of Great George Street at that time. It is true that Mr Heath was a great expansionist, and Lord Barber as he now is did what he was told by him—so I certainly would not blame him for that. But the Treasury, as far as I can recall, offered almost no resistance to those policies.

TIM CONGDON (*L. Messel & Co.*): I have my reservations about the suggestion of a secretariat, as politicians might be very confused if they were presented with an extreme variety of views. Although I agree with a lot of Alan Budd's argument I think that we have to accept that the evolution of economic policy is a very gradual process. What happens is that people are educated by events and over a period of time new rules of policy develop. As a result, the importance of the conflict of ideas is in practice removed, because certain ideas become established as the right ones.

I can illustrate that by an interpretation of how Treasury thinking about the economy has evolved since 1945. Obviously Alan Budd knows more about this than I do, but I would conjecture that, from the way in which the Treasury worked in the 'fifties and 'sixties, it was not then in favour of demand management. Throughout the 'fifties and 'sixties the rule determining fiscal policy was that the budget should be balanced above the line. The other vital consideration was that the exchange rate should be fixed. Those were the two rules, and it did not really matter what advice the Chancellor was given because ultimately those two things would override everything else. I suppose what is happening at the moment is that we are moving towards different rules—money supply rules and budget deficit rules.

I would question whether we should pay all that much attention to what economists are thinking at any particular moment. Indeed, I think it is important that the Treasury should dominate policy formation, as it will be affected by the process of education by events and become attached to certain principles and rules. This would ensure continuity in the advice Chancellors were given. That may sound very reactionary, but I am not in favour of politicians getting conflicting advice from different sources. I do not think that should be one of the inputs in the presentation of policy alternatives. But I do think having a secretariat with some people on one side and other people on the other would be terribly confusing.

BUDD: That is a politician's view—I will accept it. My proposal is in the first place to open the Treasury to a wide variety of views. As I say, different Chancellors will have different capacities to cope with uncertainty in debate. Some welcome it and others hate it. For those that hate it the Treasury will have to form a view for the Chancellor and try to persuade him of its rightness. But I am assuming that this debate is happening within the Treasury. We do not then hand over the debate to the Chancellor, particularly if he is the type of Chancellor that cannot tolerate it, as he often is.

6. Buying Out the Obstructors?

CHARLES K. ROWLEY
University of Newcastle upon Tyne

The Author

CHARLES K. ROWLEY: Professor of Economics since 1972, and Director of the Centre for Research in Public and Industrial Economics, University of Newcastle upon Tyne, since 1974. Formerly Universities of Nottingham (1962-65), Kent (1965-70), and York, (1970-72).

Author of *The British Monopolies Commission*, 1966; *Steel & Public Policy*, 1971; *Antitrust and Economic Efficiency*, 1972; (with A. T. Peacock) *Welfare Economics: A Liberal Restatement*, 1975; and many articles. For the IEA he contributed three essays, 'Public Preference for Market Processes', in *Catch '76. . .?*, Occasional Paper 'Special', No. 47, 1976, and 'Taxing in an International Labour Market', in *The State of Taxation*, Readings 16, 1977, 'Market "Failure" and Government 'Failure",' in *The Economics of Politics*, Readings 18, 1978.

Introducing Professor Rowley, Lord Robbins said:
We had, at the beginning of the morning, a paper by Professor Littlechild in which he made some critical remarks about recent trends in welfare economics. We now have the privilege of hearing one who, certainly in my judgement, has written, co-operatively, the most formidable attack on that method of approach that has appeared in the English language.[1]

I. INTRODUCTION

In 1790 the total expenditure of the public authorities in Britain accounted for approximately 12 per cent of gross national product (GNP). In 1913, despite a substantial rise in government expenditure, the total accounted for exactly the same percentage—12 per cent. Since then, dramatic changes have occurred, with the ratio rising to 50 per cent in 1971-72 and peaking at 60 per cent in 1975-76. With this increase in the economic role of the state, given the nature of the political system, the economy has been rendered increasingly vulnerable to sectional interests whose activities are extremely damaging both to aggregate economic performance and to the maintenance of fundamental individual freedoms. To identify the sectional interests and to determine how best they might be handled it is first necessary to define the precise nature of the constitutional crisis in which Britain is now placed.

The British political system is a first-past-the-post majority-vote system dominated by two major parties in which the one with a majority of seats in the House of Commons is able to intervene in the economy without any constitutional limits save for the residual influence of the now almost-defunct House of Lords. On the assumption that political parties are motivated to win votes, and that governments pursue their own objectives such as ideology, power, patronage and personal income always with a wary eye upon the probability of being re-elected, it might be thought that the prefer-

---

[1] With A. T. Peacock, *Welfare Economics: A Liberal Restatement,* Martin Robertson, 1975.

ences of the middle voter (technically the median preference voter[2]) would determine the economic role of the state. But, in reality, this tends not to be so for reasons central to this paper.

Imperfect information and uncertainty

Firstly, and most importantly, the political market-place is not characterised by perfect information concerning voter preferences over the appropriate economic role of the state. An opportunity thus presents itself for interest groups to distort information on voter preferences as a means of appropriating private benefits for their members. In particular, such opportunities are manifest in the government's own bureaucracies on which it is highly dependent for information both on the preferences of citizens and on the flexibility of its policy alternatives.

In so far as the senior bureaucrats themselves are motivated to maximise the size of their respective bureaux[3]—and this is a good proxy for many of their likely objectives such as personal income, power, patronage and the easy life—they will inevitably be driven to press for policies which require increasing government economic intervention, particularly by public expenditures but also by legislation. This process provides an inbuilt bias against the market economy, or 'capitalism', which is not always appreciated fully either by the electorate or by the politicians. It is a bias which affects decisions in both national and local government.

Incentives to organise pressure groups

Secondly, uncertainty concerning voter preferences offers an incentive to sectional interests to organise themselves into pressure groups with the aim of distorting information within the political market-place to the advantage of their memberships. It is not easy to form an effective pressure group where the benefits, if achieved,

---

[2] [Definitions of 'median preference voter' and other technical terms used by economists studying the theory of public choice, or the economics of politics, are given by Gordon Tullock in *The Vote Motive,* Hobart Paperback 9, IEA, 1976.—ED.]

[3] William A. Niskanen, *Bureaucracy: Servant or Master?,* Hobart Paperback 5, IEA, 1973.

accrue to individuals irrespective of their contributions to the campaign. The tendency of individuals to take a 'free ride' in such circumstances is strong. It is predictable, therefore, that those pressure groups most able to coerce membership and/or to induce membership *via* the 'privatisation' of benefits will dominate in the process of distorting information. Specifically, trade unions armed with the legislative privilege of the closed shop and professional groups like the doctors and the legal profession with a long tradition of professional solidarity will tend to dominate other citizens in the transmission of political information. For the most part, such groups have a clear-cut interest in expanding the economic role of the state through government expenditure and legislation.

Uncertainty is relevant also from the viewpoint of the voter. Typically, voters are not well-informed *ab initio* on the likely implications of alternative government policies, and are highly dependent upon information from those who purport to possess it. Once again both bureaucracies and powerful pressure groups have the opportunity to present information to the newspapers and broadcasting in a form favourable to their interests. Once again it will tend to be biased in favour of public intervention. Politicians, national and local, with an interest in wielding power, have little or no short-term incentive to disabuse the voters of such bias, even where they recognise its existence.

Government behaviour and pressure-group intimidation

The presence within the British economy of powerful, highly-protected pressure groups provides further opportunities to distort the behaviour of government through the intimidation of voters. By threatening to inflict harm on others in the absence of a favourable political response, or even by inflicting such harm, trade unions and professional organisations may shift voter preferences in such manner as to appropriate significant economic gains.

Although in principle it might appear that such behaviour would not necessarily bias government in favour of intervention, in practice the bias does exist. For the trade unions and professional groups within the non-trading public sector, like education and medicine, and even to a lesser extent in the trading public sector, like transport and fuel, are usually protected by statute from private competition, and moreover are protected by security of tenure from the economic costs of their behaviour. In contrast, equivalent organisations within the private sector are relatively constrained by the fear of inducing bankruptcies or a major loss of jobs as a consequence of intimidatory action. Thus it is that a large public sector itself sows the seeds for continuing expansion relative to the private sector.

II. THE NATURE OF THE CONSTITUTIONAL CRISIS

The political system in Britain in recent years has become excessively vulnerable to powerful interest groups—notably the public sector trade unions and professional organisations as well as government bureaucracy—which together wield immense economic power largely because they have been given monopoly power by statute. These groups, in the pursuit of unenlightened short-term self-interest, have imposed upon Britain a public sector which is excessive in scale, excessively bureaucratised, producer- rather than consumer-minded, over-manned, over-remunerated, and generally characterised by very low productivity. With government expenditure accounting for more than 50 per cent of gross national product, and with the private sector suffering from high taxation, from the crowding-out of its own investment programmes and from an inadequate social infrastructure,[4] it is not surprising that Britain is rapidly heading towards a position of comparative under-development, and that British citizens are fast losing such important liberties as freedom of choice of occupation and consumption which have long been viewed as the hallmarks of British civilisation.

At least one of the major political parties in Britain now recognises the nature of this constitutional crisis. The issue to which this paper addresses itself is how such a party, elected to office on a voter mandate for reform, might best proceed to an effective solution.

III. SHOULD THE OBSTRUCTORS COLLECTIVELY BE BOUGHT OUT?

It is fundamental to human nature that people who have acquired 'rights' or who have seized 'advantages' are seldom happy to sacrifice their gains in the absence of compensation. There has been much discussion, therefore, about the possibility of buying out collectively the most powerful of the potential obstructors, particularly within the union sector (or at least of buying out 'legitimate' expectations such as the right to strike). Should such powerful public sector employees as the Forces, the miners, the power workers, the police, the firemen, the doctors, even perhaps the ambulancemen and the sewage workers be offered bribes in the form of guarantees of high relative remuneration in return for loss of or absence of the right to strike? Such a policy is now viewed favourably by a range of political opinion. In my view it is fundamentally misguided, most especially for employees in the non-trading public sector, especially in education and the health services.

Constitutional objections

Such a policy would have serious implications for those who endorse the constitutional position that there should be no taxation without representation. To a considerable extent the incomes of people who are employed in the non-trading public sector (and to a lesser extent in the trading public sector) are paid with revenues derived from taxes which individual citizens are not allowed to evade. To guarantee incomes in the public sector, therefore, is effectively to eliminate taxpayer control over the level of taxation. Britain lost a colony by such behaviour only two centuries ago. Even if the strike-threat were to be replaced by compulsory arbitration, taxpayer control would still be jeopardised, since the arbitrator would effectively determine the level of taxation by awarding pay without reference to tax-payers, especially in a country such as Britain in which it is costly or even impossible to lay off labour as a means of controlling the amount of public expenditure.

Furthermore, even if the constitutional issue is ignored on grounds of expediency, serious problems of three kinds remain concerning the collective buying-out of obstructors. Firstly, even if the leaders of trade unions in the public sector agreed to a deal, it is far from self-evident that they would always be able to honour it in the face of shopfloor rebellion. Clearly, a system of enforceable penalties for breach of contract would be required *de minimis* as part of such a policy.

Secondly, what price should be paid? Where in the wages hierarchy would the various public employees be slotted in? What mechanism might there be for re-negotiating the hierarchy to reflect changing conditions of supply and demand? Or are such conditions to be ignored in the name of expediency? Finally, what are the likely consequences of buying out extortion? Will the extortionists, flushed with the success of their threats, merely increase their demands and secure, as part of a re-negotiated deal, a yet more powerful position from which to intimidate society? The history of the 'social contract' between the unions and the last Labour Government offers no encouragement whatsoever for the Danegeld solution.

IV. TOWARDS A CONSTITUTIONAL SETTLEMENT

In one sense the title of this conference, 'The Taming of Government', is misleading. In my view, the growth of the public sector, given the political system, has weakened rather than strengthened government, both central and local. The crisis thereby induced is essentially a constitutional crisis which will be resolved, if at all, only by constitutional reform. Paradoxically, if government in Britain is to regain effective control over the British economy it will do so only by severely curtailing its economic activities and restricting its constitutional powers.

The problem of the public sector in Britain is largely an outcome of the unrestricted powers of government combined with the adoption throughout the post-war period of Keynesian demand-management policies. For, as Professor James Buchanan has shrewdly observed,[4] the pressures of the political market-place have introduced a fiscal bias in favour of the budget deficit, irrespective of demand management considerations in almost all countries which have abandoned the balanced-budget principle. The explanation is to be found in the directly identifiable nature of those who gain from increased public expenditure and reduced taxation in comparison with the more pervasive but less visible benefits from lower public expenditure and/ or higher taxation. The direct beneficiaries will lobby; the indirect will not; and the policy of the budget deficit will be politically seductive.

---

[4] In *The Consequences of Mr Keynes,* with R. E. Wagner and John Burton, Hobart Paper 78, IEA, 1978.

Curtailing the growth/power of public sector workers

The consequence of continuing budget deficits is a growing public sector with all the power it implies for bureaucracies, public-sector trade unions, and professional organisations. If such power is to be curtailed, therefore, the fiscal bias must be controlled. Any government in office, however, will face the pressure of a pro-deficit lobby and, in terms of public choice theory,[5] it is predictable that in the long term it will succumb. The solution therefore proposed in this paper is that any incoming reformist government should make a prior constitutional resolution that the budget must balance and use the size of the budget to control aggregate demand by the balanced-budget multiplier. By so doing, governments will avoid political odium every time they attempt to reduce the size—absolutely or relatively—of the public sector, and will face the immediate tax costs of raising the amount of public expenditure.

If such a constitutional rule were to be accompanied by a monetary rule designed to limit the rate of growth of the money supply to the rate of growth of productivity (once inflation was brought under control), the ability of sectional interests to use the rate of inflation as an instrument for income redistribution would be eliminated.

Market constraints on government employees

From such a strong constitutional position, a reformist government would be much better placed than at present to resolve the public sector problem. The approach should essentially be that of undermining the power of public sector employees whilst re-introducing market constraints wherever possible. There are several closely related strands to such a policy.

First, statutory prohibitions on competition from the private sector should be withdrawn in all public sector commodities save those involving the provision of law and order and the defence of the realm. Clearly, where (as in defence) additional natural monopoly characteristics are strong, labour market competition will not be marked. But relatively few public sector commodities fall into that category. Central and local governments should then be encouraged to ignore their bureaucracies and allow taxpayers credits where they

---

[5] An outline of this theory, which in Britain is called the economics of politics, will be found in Gordon Tullock, *The Vote Motive, op. cit.,* and in *The Economics of Politics,* IEA Readings 18, 1978, especially the introductory essay by Professor Buchanan.

purchase publicly non-traded goods such as education and medicine in non-public markets. In due course, public provision would be curtailed where private provision proved dominant, and public sector charges might be introduced, rather than taxes paid, where market viability was established and the public sector survived. In such ways, cuts in real public expenditure could occur without any loss in the volume and with gains in the quality of these commodities.

Secondly, the government might consider buying *individual employees* out of their unions where the latter had depressed wages by policies of over-manning or under-capitalisation. Particularly in industries or occupations characterised by technical change, such a policy might be very attractive to erstwhile individual unionists, even though it would clearly engender bitter union resistance. *The Times* newspaper is a private sector example of such a policy attempt. Even if the right to join a union were to be retained by those who abandoned their unions for higher pay, detailed productivity and manning requirements unlikely to be endorsed by an existing union could be drafted into the conditions of employment.

Thirdly, the rights to strike and to picket should be withdrawn from all public sector employees. It is for the voter *via* representative government to determine rates of pay in the public sector. The right to strike was originally granted because of the apparent conflict between capitalist and worker, not because of conflict between the worker and the state. Public employee unions which ignored the law and engaged in strike activity might be rendered liable in tort for damages; and the individual strikers and their families would have no recourse to the social security system. The right to strike in the public sector gives employees an unjustified and privileged influence over the rate of national taxation and the quantity of local rates. An independent information agency might be established to draw comparisons between pay and productivity in the private and public sectors so that taxpayer/rate-payer voters have access to relevant information.

V. IS SUCH CONSTITUTIONAL REFORM FEASIBLE?

The short answer, within the context of the existing political system, is that I do not know. Certainly, those among the bureaucracies, unions and professional organisations who saw in such reforms the end of their power and the loss of such rents as they might have been extracting would bitterly oppose every one of these proposals. But the public sector unions remain a minority within the union movement, and unionists are still a minority of the voting public. Britain remains a democracy.

Moreover, although this paper has centred attention upon the public sector, where the chief obstructors reside, it would be essential within the private sector to restore competition in commodity markets by antitrust and withdrawal of all government subsidies, to limit severely the role of picketing, to reduce state financial support to the families of people on strike, and to eliminate the closed shop. Such measures might be viewed by public sector employees as a *quid pro quo* for their own loss of privileges. In a country as conflict-ridden as Britain now appears to be, there are some gains from trade to be obtained in measures designed to reduce the intimidatory powers of rival unions.

Alternatives to constitutional reform?

What, then, if such constitutional reform should fail? Is there another way? The answer must be that there are several. One would be for government to move towards hyper-inflation in Latin-American style as a means of delaying a political solution. A second is for government to continue with policies such as those of the last Labour Government, accepting a high degree of labour market conflict, relative impoverishment and massive state intervention. Yet a third is for democracy to be sacrificed in the name of economic efficiency and for Britain to be ruled by the gun.

Such a solution, however unpalatable, cannot be ruled out if labour market violence escalates at all in Britain during the next few critically important years. It is better by far, however, to experiment with constitutional reform designed to re-introduce market constraints on the exercise of power both in the commodity and in the labour and capital markets, and to restore a close relationship between earnings and productivity. That is the only hope for the survival of democracy in Britain in the longer term.

BIBLIOGRAPHY

[1] Buchanan, J. M., 'From Private Preferences to Public Philosophy: The Development of Public Choice', in *The Economics of Politics,* IEA Readings 18, IEA, 1978.

[2] Buchanan, J. M., Burton, J., and Wagner, R. E., *The Conse-quences of Mr Keynes,* Hobart Paper 78, IEA, 1978.

[3] Rowley, C. K., 'Market "Failure" and Government "Failure" ', in *The Economics of Politics* (reference 1).

[4] Rowley, C. K., 'Liberalism and Collective Choice', *National Westminster Bank Review,* May 1979.

Questions and Discussion

C. A. K. FENN-SMITH (*M. & G. Group*): I am very much in agreement with Professor Rowley, but I am a little perplexed by one attitude. He lumped together the public sector unions and professional associations. By professional associations in this context does he mean professional bodies, largely doctors and lawyers?

PROF. ROWLEY: Yes, but lawyers less so because their tradition is not to be collectively powerful. I am thinking of very powerful groups such as doctors, for example, who would not call themselves unionists but are a professional organisation, very well organised, well drilled, and able to put very considerable pressure upon governments of any political complexion. In many ways one might have seen the doctors as leading the last round of battles on the pay front. I am not concerned only with people who would class themselves as members of the Trades Union Congress but organisations that nevertheless wield a lot of power but which are outside that grouping.

DR RALPH HORWITZ (*London Regional Management Centre*): Pro-fessor W. H. Hutt, my old professor at just about the end of the war, published a book called *Plan for Reconstruction.*[1] He specifically proposed the buying out of restrictive practices—it was more particularly related to union practice at the time. The job one does is today perceived as a property right whose duration is determined by oneself without regard to any market determination of the value related to the output. In the light of the growth of redundancy payments, etc., it would seem there are major dangers in giving further weight to the idea that there is such a notion of property right. I particularly welcome Professor Rowley's em-phasis on what I would regard as political economy as distinct from economics and econometrics. The way to bring about a significant im-provement is to go back to writing books on political economy and, with

---

[1] Kegan Paul, 1943.

great respect, no further attempt should be made to construct ever more sophisticated models of economic behaviour. At heart these are problems of political economy, and one cannot in any meaningful way separate the politics from the economics.

ROWLEY: In considering the constitution and the restraints on government one has to relate the two together in terms of political economy. I would distinguish between two fundamental issues, where detailed modelling is probably damaging—you lose sight of the wood for the trees. But there is still a very valuable role for detailed econometric work in analysing in particular the behaviour of markets or the behaviour of the economy as a whole. I would not want to work on the basis of fundamental ignorance, because there is no way you can move forward on that basis. I would distinguish the two. But for fundamental issues I think the return to political economy is very important. The separation of economics and politics during the past half-century has not done a lot of good for economics itself. A lot of unrealistic proposals have been put forward by economists because they have not perceived the pressures and stresses on politicians. This is exactly the objection to Keynes. His *General Theory* was written as if *he* would be operating the economy. It is an élitist view of public policy—Keynes would see himself as responding to economic signals. What he failed to perceive was that politicians respond to *political* signals, and of course that process reaches very different results. Economists generally have been guilty of that error. They have not seen that there is a political market-place where the signals may be very different from the economic signals—and politicians are going to react to the political signals.

R. C. SANSOM (*Contractors' Plant Association*): On the control of monetary growth, would you for example disarm the Treasury by seeking to alter its relationship with the Bank of England and to establish the Bank in a position somewhat closer to that in the American system, where it is not so easy to monkey about with the printing of currency?

ROWLEY: Yes. In principle I suppose the Bank of England still has some residual right to control the money supply, but I would convert it to the sort of system that the Federal Reserve Bank operates. That separation, enshrined with the constitutional rule, would give much more power to government. Government could then say 'We cannot do this, we are not in a position to deliver', which governments must sometimes wish they could say. Why did we need the IMY to put our house in order?—because, not having a written constitution, we wanted someone else to take responsibility for the control of the economy. Why did some politicians want to get into the European Snake?—because they wanted the Germans to run our economy for us, and if we were tied to the

Deutschmark they would have been in a much more powerful position to allow that to happen. Some politicians would like to have their powers restricted. The difficulty is to get an elected government with a large enough majority to take a long term view and say 'Yes, we will refrain from meddling in return for a constitutional settlement that you do not meddle with us.' But does our political system allow victorious politicians to act with that degree of foresight?

PROF. A. P. L. MINFORD (*University of Liverpool*): Do I understand by your constitutional suggestion that you are being literal, or are you suggesting a variety of possible formulas because I was a little puzzled? You said that the balanced-budget multiplier could be used for demand management.

ROWLEY: Partly.

MINFORD: I am a little concerned because I think the balanced-budget multiplier is probably zero.

ROWLEY: A lot of what I am saying depends on a fundamental belief that the market system would be more stable in unemployment and inflation than the intervention system we have at the moment. Any power that you take away from government does, of course, reduce its ability to fine tune. And at the limit, it may reduce it entirely. Fundamentally I believe that the market system, although it would not be totally stable, would be more likely to achieve price stability with high employment if a government was constrained in these ways.

MINFORD: It seems to me there is a slight problem in your approach; you are effectively getting rid of all the traditional stabilisers, such as, for example, the stabilisation of tax revenues. If a large shock hit the economy, you would have tax rates raised in response in order to balance the budget. That seems to me to be a little risky and likely to lead to considerably greater variance. I wonder whether it is more reasonable to suggest that certain rules be considered, like stabilisers, for example, as being acceptable and to define the relevant operational criteria. Once you have defined these operational criteria, they could in some way be entrenched, so that the normal published stabilisation rules operate, like the tax stabiliser, for example, and that would be the entrenched constitutional clause, rather than the idea that the actual budget should be balanced on a year-by-year basis. In other words, this would imply that the average budget, or the longer-run budget should be balanced, or the longer-run money supply.

There are tremendous problems in defining the money supply rules to be adhered to on a very short-term basis. And even on a six-months basis there may be problems with shifting among the money functions, and so on. I wonder whether the more promising avenue might not be to try and consider published formulae that would bind government, not to put knowledge into the system, but to follow rules around these on target.

ROWLEY: People who would put forward a balanced-budget criterion would inevitably make a constitutional provision for allowing it to be broken in a state of emergency. Or something of that kind. One could have emergency procedures with careful rules as to what constituted an emergency.

The other way out is to devise rules to ameliorate the harsher implications of a very tight constitutional rule. My worry there is that all the loopholes open up and all the opportunities for manipulation, and I suspect that in the end, you would have to revert to fine tuning. I would prefer a simple constitutional rule which might be rather harsh under certain circumstances, but would have an emergency provision. If we could get perfect rules, I would be happy, but I fear that even flexible rules would all be open-ended and routes out would emerge.

MINFORD: But if they were entrenched rules and very precisely defined, and only subject to constitutional over-ruling by two-thirds majority or something, maybe this would . . .

ROWLEY: I would not want to rule it out. It is an interesting deviant or alternative to my proposal, but . . .

PROF. IVOR PEARCE (*University of Southampton*): One thing that might be more desirable than government built-in stabilisers would be free enterprise rules or stabilisers. It is, I am sure, not beyond the wit of economists to devise a way of making it profitable to annihilate money when there is a crisis arising from its increase. And to remove entirely from the government and from the banks any right whatever to create money without the co-operation of individual profit-makers. I think we need to restore the situation to something like it was when we had gold, because you could not create gold, you had to get down on your hands and knees and dig for it, at a cost. And therefore prices in terms of gold varied because they were determined by labour costs. It is possible to devise such a scheme, but it's a long story.

ROWLEY: Hayek has argued the case for denationalising the money supply,[2] and I think there are arguments for it. The gold standard, too, was very important. Not only did we lose the balanced-budget principle as a result of Keynes, but almost simultaneously the gold standard. And we then moved to a sort of creeping fixed exchange rate system that has now gone into a 'dirty' float. Government has acquired an extra dimension

---

[2] *Denationalisation of Money: The Argument Refined,* Hobart Paper 70, IEA, 2nd Edition, 1978.

121

of freedom now because we have been losing implicit constitutional rules over the last 25 years.

PEARCE: The point I was going to make just now is that there really was a revolution in the attitudes of the Treasury—it began to gather ground perhaps in the late 1930s. Everyone used to complain about the Treasury: 'The Treasury is awful', they complained, 'they never let us spend anything.' And there was a great tradition that it was politicians who wanted to spend and the Treasury who stopped them from doing it. But since Keynes, the Treasury wants to drive the bus itself. And I thought that that was what this Seminar was all about—whether we could get the driver off the bus.

ROWLEY: If you have a balanced-budget principle, this will force the Chancellor of the Exchequer to state his spending plans simultaneously with his taxation plans. That has not been the tradition in this country. The budget has been concerned with taxes, and the public expenditure programmes were dribbled out over a period, and there was no attempt to pull the two together at the time the budget was being prepared'.

PEARCE: I would want to amend that very slightly. There may be a case for some public authority engaging in productive activity and thereby creating capital. What you have to stop them doing is borrowing money against bonds and then frittering it away.

OLIVER STUTCHBURY: How far does Professor Rowley think the power of the obstructors is based on the extreme centralisation of government in this country? People elected to local authorities have no say whatsoever over the pay of their employees: it is all decided centrally. Until you get some sort of competition in local pay, these people will continue to obstruct. The simplest way of stopping them from obstructing would be a break-up of government, so that decisions about pay would be taken by local councillors who were meant to be elected to look after this business.

ROWLEY: I entirely agree. I think that one of the under-estimated qualities of the German constitution, what has made it so successful, is its federal nature. That system, together with proportional representation, has severely weakened this central clashing of powerful bodies which is such a feature of the British economy. It would be an enormous help if we could get decentralisation of that kind, particularly if it were linked with the abolition of the statutory monopoly. Local government employees' are able to inflict such pain because they have a statutory monopoly. If the post workers will not deliver the mail, then, unless you arrange illegal schemes, you cannot move the mail. There is no reason at all, in a situation like that, why private contractors should not be hired. And this competition would weaken the postal workers' bargaining positions. So there are a number of political reforms which could be considered.

The real worry is that if, for example, a new government with a reformist mandate came into office, if it did not put some controls on its own position, I would not give it much prospect of doing much more than the present Government can do, faced with this kind of pressure-group and bureaucratic restriction. It seems to me that they ought to say to themselves: 'Right, now we know what is going on, we know where the pressures are going to come, therefore we must do our best to neutralise them in advance.' You are then much more likely to be able to move forward with a policy which could be politically successful.

LORD ROBBINS: We reach the last item on the programme, a vote of thanks to the speakers by Mr Gordon Richards.

GORDON RICHARDS (*Hammersmith and West London College*): I wish to express our collective thanks, Lord Robbins, for your generosity in chairing our proceedings today. One continues to be awed by your intellectual acuity, your continued lucidity of style and elegance of manner, which has been exhibited in your many writings over the years. I wish that many contemporary economists would attempt to emulate these qualities. You have presided over IEA seminars in the past—and you always add lustre to our proceedings.

May I also express our thanks to the speakers from America, Liverpool, Birmingham, Newcastle and Sevenoaks, who have made their long and heavily subsidised journeys either by British Airways or British Rail, to be with us today. We have benefited from them all. Thank you very much. (*Applause.*)

LORD ROBBINS: Thank you very much indeed, Mr Richards. I certainly had no suspicion at all when I called on you to move the vote of thanks that you were going to speak about my humble function of sitting in this chair. I assure you that I regard that as a very great privilege and now, as always, when I come to IEA meetings, I go away with my head full of things which have not occurred to me before—and tremendous admiration for Arthur Seldon, Ralph Harris, John Wood and all their helpers, who, without a scrap of public subsidy, have succeeded in bringing about one of the most notable movements of public opinion of my very long lifetime. I thank Arthur and his friends very much indeed for inviting me and thank you all for coming and participating on this very interesting occasion.

List of Participants at IEA Seminar on the Taming of Government *(6 April 1979)*

BALMAR, P. E., *De La Rue*
BARCLAY, CLIFFORD
BARRON, SIR DONALD, *Rowntree Mackintosh*
BISHOP, R. K., *Phoenix*
DU BOULAY, MISS LOUISE, *Consolidated Goldfields*
BRACEWELL-MILNES, DR J. B., *Erasmus College, Rotterdam*
BRITTAN, SAMUEL, *Financial Times*
BRITTON, A. J. C., *Treasury*
BUDD, DR ALAN, *London Graduate School of Business Studies*
BURNS, PROFESSOR TERRY, *London Graduate School of Business Studies*
BUTLER, I. G., *Lead Industries Group*
BUTLER, DR EAMONN, *Adam Smith Institute*
BURTON, JOHN, *Kingston Polytechnic*

CAIRNCROSS, MISS FRANCES, *Guardian*
CAVE, MRS MERRIE, *Hammersmith & West London College*
CONGDON, TIM, *L. Messel & Co.*

FALCONER, J. A. R., *Scottish Eastern*
FAIRBAIRN, J. S., *M & G Group*
FENN-SMITH, C. A. K., *M. & G. Group*

GASTER, JOHN, *Williams & Glyn's Bank*
GOULD, PROF. JULIUS, *University of Nottingham*
GOODSALL, W. A. R., *National Provident Institution*
GORTON, J. E., *B.P. Oil*
GRAY, D., *Dept. of Social Services, City University*

HALSTEAD, R. T., *Beecham Group*
HARWOOD, JOHN, *Philips Industries*
HARRIS, W. C., *Phoenix Assurance*
HEFFERNAN, JOHN, *United Newspapers*
HOFF, OLE-JACOB, *Farmand, Oslo, Norway*
HORWITZ, DR RALPH, *London Regional Management Centre*

JACKSON, C. M., *Spillers*
JOHNSON, CHRISTOPHER, *Lloyds Bank*

KEEVIL, A. C. A., *Fitch Lovell*

LEES, PROF. DENNIS, *University of Nottingham*
LINGLE, DR CHRISTOPHER
LOOMBE, R. C., *Rank Hovis McDougall*
LITTLECHILD, PROF. S. C., *University of Birmingham*

MARGOLIS, CECIL, *C. Margolis (Harrogate) Ltd.*
MEAKIN, J. CHRISTOPHER
MILNE, ADAM BRUCE, *Newsday, BBC*
MINFORD, PROF. A. P. L., *University of Liverpool*
MYDDELTON, PROF. D. R., *Cranfield School of Management*

NISSEN, GEORGE, *Stock Exchange*

ORCHARD, LAWRENCE, *Ever Ready*

PAPPS, IVY, *University of Durham*
PEARCE, PROF. IVOR, *University of Southampton*
PIRIE, DR MADSEN, *Adam Smith Institute*

RANDALL, L. D., *Fitch Lovell*
RACKHAM, PETER, *BAT Industries*
REEKIE, DR DUNCAN, *University of Edinburgh*
REED, C. J., *C. Margolis (Harrogate) Ltd.*
RICHARDS, GORDON, *Hammersmith & West London College*
ROBBINS, LORD
ROWLES, RON, *Ever Ready*
ROWLEY, PROF. CHARLES, *University of Newcastle*
RYBCZYNSKI, T. M., *Lazard Bros.*

SANDFORD, PROF. CEDRIC, *University of Bath*
SANSOM, R. C., *Contractors Plant Association*
SCANLAN, A. F. G., *B.P. Oil*
SELDON, MRS MARJORIE, *Friends of the Educational Voucher Experiment in Representative Regions (F.E.V.E.R.)*
SHENFIELD, MRS B. E.
STUTCHBURY, OLIVER
SUTHERLAND, B. W., *Harris & Sheldon Group*
SYMONS, E. J., *BAT Industries*

TEDBURY, S., *Tate & Lyle*
TULLOCK, PROF. GORDON, *Virginia Polytechnic Institute and State University*

WHITAKER, P. E., *Amoco*
WILLIAMS, A. F., *Guardian Royal*
WILSON, SIR REGINALD, *Transport Development Group*
WATHEN, J. P. G., *Barclays Bank*

Author Index

Subject Index

129

130

IEA READINGS

1. Education—A Framework for Choice
Papers on historical, economic and administrative aspects of choice in education and its finance
A. C. F. Beales, Mark Blaug, E. G. West, Sir Douglas Veale, *with an Appraisal by* Dr Rhodes Boyson
1967   Second Edition 1970 (xvi+100pp., 90p)

2. Growth through Industry
A re-consideration of principles and practice before and after the National Plan
John Jewkes, Jack Wiseman, Ralph Harris, John Brunner, Richard Lynn, and seven company chairmen
1967   (xiii+157pp., £1·00)

4. Taxation—A Radical Approach
A re-assessment of the high level of British taxation and the scope for its reduction
Vito Tanzi, J. B. Bracewell-Milnes, D. R. Myddelton
1970   (xii+130pp., 90p)

5. Economic Issues in Immigration
An exploration of the liberal approach to public policy on immigration
Charles Wilson, W. H. Hutt, Sudha Shenoy, David Collard, E. J. Mishan, Graham Hallett, *with an Introduction by* Sir Arnold Plant
1970   (xviii+155pp., £1·25)

6. Inflation and the Unions
Three studies on the effects of labour monopoly power in Britain and the USA
Gottfried Haberler, Michael Parkin, Henry Smith
1972   (xii+88pp.; available on microfiche only: £3·50)

7. Verdict on Rent Control
Essays on the economic consequences of political action to restrict rents in five countries
F. A. Hayek, Milton Friedman and George Stigler, Bertrand de Jouvenel, F. W. Paish, Sven Rydenfelt, *with an Introduction by* F. G. Pennance
1972   (xvi+80pp., £1·00)

8. Inflation: Economy and Society
Twelve papers by economists, businessmen and politicians on causes, consequences, cures
Lord Robbins, Brian Griffiths, J. A. P. Treasure, D. R. Myddelton, Raymond Fletcher, Paul Bareau, Henry Smith, Andrew Alexander, Richard Lynn, Lewis Whyte, Nicholas Ridley, Graham Hutton
1972   (ix+136pp.; available on microfiche only: £3·50)

9. The Long Debate on Poverty
Eight essays on industrialisation and 'the condition of England'
R. M. Hartwell, G. E. Mingay, Rhodes Boyson, Norman McCord,
C. G. Hanson, A. W. Coats, W. H. Chaloner and W. O. Henderson,
J. M. Jefferson
Second Edition with an introductory essay on 'The State of the Debate'
by Norman Gash
1974   (xxxii+243pp., £2·50)

10.   Mergers, Take-overs, and the Structure of Industry
Ten papers on economics, law, rules
G. C. Allen, M. E. Beesley, Harold Edey, Brian Hindley,
Sir Anthony Burney, Peter Cannon, Ian Fraser, Lord Shawcross,
Sir Geoffrey Howe, Lord Robbins
1973   (ix+92pp., £1·00)

11.   Regional Policy For Ever?
Essays on the history, theory and political economy of forty years of
'regionalism'
Graham Hallett, Peter Randall, E. G. West
1973   (xii+152pp., £1·80)

12.   The Economics of Charity
Essays on the comparative economics and ethics of giving and selling,
with applications to blood
Armen A. Alchian and William R. Allen, Michael H. Cooper,
Anthony J. Culyer, Marilyn J. Ireland, Thomas R. Ireland,
David B. Johnson, James Koch, A. J. Salsbury, Gordon Tullock
1974   (xviii+197pp., £2·00)

13.   Government and the Land
Does state control help or hinder? Is town planning necessary?
Does land speculation intensify inflation? Is nationalisation the cure?
A. A. Walters, F. G. Pennance, W. A. West, D. R. Denman,
Barry Bracewell-Milnes, S. E. Denman, D. G. Slough, Stuart Ingram
1974   (xiii+95pp.; available on microfiche only: £3·50)

14.   Inflation: Causes, Consequences, Cures
Discourses on the debate between the monetary and trade union
interpretations
Lord Robbins, Samuel Brittan, A. W. Coats, Milton Friedman, Peter Jay,
David Laidler
With an Addendum by F. A. Hayek
1974   3rd Impression 1976   (vii+120pp., £2·00)

15.   The Dilemmas of Government Expenditure
Essays in political economy by economists and parliamentarians
Robert Bacon and Walter Eltis, Tom Wilson, Jack Wiseman,
David Howell, David Marquand, John Pardoe, Richard Lynn
1976   (xi+110pp., £2·00)

16. The State of Taxation
A. R. Prest, Colin Clark, Walter Elkan, Charles K. Rowley,
Barry Bracewell-Milnes, Ivor F. Pearce
Comments by Geoffrey E. Wood, Alun G. Davies, Nigel Lawson,
T. W. Hutchison, Alan T. Peacock, Michael Moohr, Malcolm R. Fisher,
George Psacharopoulos, Dennis Lees, J. S. Flemming, Douglas Eden
with an Address by Lord Houghton
1977   (xvi+116pp., £2·00)

17. Trade Unions: Public Goods or Public 'Bads'?
Lord Robbins, Charles G. Hanson, John Burton, Cyril Grunfeld, Brian
Griffiths, Alan Peacock
Commentaries by Peter Mathias, Norman McCord, P. J. Sloane,
J. T. Addison, Martin Ricketts, George Yarrow, Charles T. Rowley,
Dennis Lees, Harry Ferns, Keith Hartley, Reg Prentice, Jo Grimond
with an Address by Lord Scarman
1978   (xiv+134pp., £2·00)

18. The Economics of Politics
See page 136

19. City Lights
Essays on financial institutions and markets in the City of London
E. Victor Morgan, R. A. Brealey, B. S. Yamey, Paul Bareau
1979   (x+70pp., £1·50)

20. Job 'Creation'—or Destruction?
Six essays on the effects of government intervention in the labour market
John Addison, Christian Watrin, Malcolm R. Fisher, Albert Rees,
Yukihide Okano and Mitsuake Okabe, Walter Eltis *with an introductory essay by* Ralph Harris
1979   (xiii+149pp., £3·00)

For further information about IEA publications and details of subscription services, etc., please write to:

THE INSTITUTE OF ECONOMIC AFFAIRS
2 Lord North Street, Westminster, London SW1P 3LB

SOME IEA PAPERS ON
THE ECONOMICS OF POLITICS

Readings 18
The Economics of Politics
JAMES M. BUCHANAN, CHARLES K. ROWLEY, ALBERT BRETON,
JACK WISEMAN, BRUNO FREY, A. T. PEACOCK, and seven other
contributors. Introduced by JO GRIMOND
1978   (xiii+194pp., £3·00)
'. . . bureaucrats are seen as trying to increase the size of their staff and
the responsibilities of their departments, in much the same way as a
small businessman strives to increase his profits.
'Politicians . . . have other goals. They are basically bidding for votes
. . . They will also . . . try to outbid each other with promises of good
things to the electorate. This—the theory argues—is an inevitable
consequence of the way democracies take decisions.'
Frances Cairncross, *Guardian*

Hobart Paper 78
The Consequences of Mr Keynes
JAMES M. BUCHANAN, JOHN BURTON and R. E. WAGNER
1978   2nd Impression 1979   (94pp., £1·50)
'In order to provide against irresponsible budget deficit financing, the
authors of the booklet call for a written rule for the British Parliament
that there should be no budget deficit.'
Leader in *Yorkshire Post*

Hobart Paperback 9
The Vote Motive
GORDON TULLOCK
with a Commentary by Morris Perlman
1976   2nd Impression 1978   (xvi+88pp., £1·50)
'Professor Tullock's tract deserves our attention because it is disturbing,
as it is meant to be. It invites us to consider further what we should be
constantly considering—those comfortable assumptions about our
institutions that prompt us to shy away from changes that might be
beneficial. There is more in common between the public and private
sectors than most of us are willing to allow.'   *Municipal Journal*

Hobart Paperback 5
Bureaucracy: Servant or Master?
WILLIAM A. NISKANEN
with Commentaries by
**Douglas Houghton, Maurice Kogan, Nicholas Ridley and Ian
Senior**
1973   (xii+103pp., £1·00)
'Niskanen argues, with some cogency, that every kind of pressure on a
bureau head leads him to maximise his budget.'
Peter Wilsher, *Sunday Times*